ENCYCLOPEDIA OF GOOD HEALTH

STRESS AND MENTAL HEALTH

ENCYCLOPEDIA OF GOOD HEALTH

STRESS AND MENTAL HEALTH

Series Editors

MARIO ORLANDI, Ph.D., M.P.H.

and

DONALD PRUE, Ph.D.

Text by

ANNETTE SPENCE

Facts On File Publications
New York • Oxford

A FRIEDMAN GROUP BOOK

Copyright © 1988 by Michael Friedman Publishing Group, Inc.

All rights reserved. No part of this book may be reproduced or utilized in any form or by any means, electronic, mechanical, photocopying, recording or by any information storage and retrieval systems, without the prior written permission of the copyright owner.

First published in 1988 by Facts On File Publications, Inc.
460 Park Avenue South
New York, New York 10016

Library of Congress Cataloging-in-Publication Data

Spence, Annette.
Stress and mental health.

(Encyclopedia of good health)
Includes index.
1. Stress (Psychology) 2. Mental health. I. Title. II. Series.
BF575.S75S69   1988   155.9   87-20092
ISBN 0-8160-1668-2

British CIP data available upon request

ENCYCLOPEDIA OF GOOD HEALTH: STRESS AND MENTAL HEALTH
was prepared and produced by
Michael Friedman Publishing Group, Inc.
15 West 26th Street
New York, New York 10010

Designer: Rod Gonzalez
Art Director: Mary Moriarty
Illustrations: Kenneth Spengler

Typeset by BPE Graphics, Inc.
Color separated, printed, and bound in Hong Kong by South Seas International Press Company Ltd.

1 3 5 7 9 10 8 6 4 2

About the Series Editors

Mario Orlandi is chief of the Division of Health Promotion Research of the American Health Foundation. He has a Ph.D. in psychology with further study in health promotion. He has written and edited numerous books and articles, among them The American Health Foundation Guide to Lifespan Health *(Dodd Mead, 1984), and has received numerous grants, awards, and commendations. Orlandi lives in New York City.*

Dr. Donald M. Prue is a management consultant specializing in productivity improvement and wellness programs in business and industrial settings. He was formerly a senior scientist at the American Health Foundation and holds a doctorate in clinical psychology. He has published over forty articles and books on health promotion and was recognized in the Congressional Record *for his work. Prue lives in Houston, Texas.*

About the Author

Annette Spence received a degree in journalism from the University of Tennessee at Knoxville. Her articles have appeared in Redbook, Weight Watchers Magazine, Cosmopolitan, *and* Bride's, *and she has contributed to a number of books. Spence is associate editor for Whittle Communications, a health media company in New York City. She lives in Stamford, Connecticut.*

CONTENTS

How to Use This Book · page 9

PART I

What's Important For Me To Know About Stress and Mental Health? · page 11

Stress Is a Natural, Necessary Life Function · page 12

Fight-or-Flight · page 12
Modern Stress · page 19

Stressors Come in All Shapes, Sizes, and Forms · page 22

School · page 22
Friends · page 22
Boyfriends and Girlfriends · page 25
Family · page 26
Daily Problems · page 29
Big Changes · page 30
Environment · page 30
Physical Stressors · page 30
Chemical Stressors · page 35
Other Stressors · page 35

Prolonged Stress Causes Health Problems · page 43

Stress Signals · page 43
Breakdowns · page 53
Physical Illnesses and Disorders · page 53
Mood Disorders · page 57

How to Help Someone Who Shows the Suicide Signals · page 59

How to Handle the Suicide of Someone You Know · page 60

E N T S

PART II

What Can I Do To Control My Stress? · page 69

The Change-It Solution · page 70

General Stress-Avoidance Tactics · page 72
Organizing Smarts · page 73
Being a Good Judge · page 74
How to Say "No" · page 76
Facing Up to What You Really Can't Change · page 77

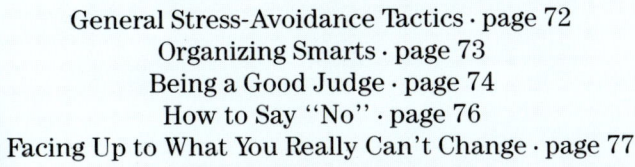

The Mind-Over-Matter Solution · page 79

The Go-With-It Solution · page 82

Exercise · page 82
Breathing and Stretching · page 84
Daydreaming · page 87
People Support · page 89
Write Your Own Relaxation Plan · page 94
Mismanaging Stress · page 94

Can You Do It? · page 95

Stressor Directory · page 100

Staying in Control · page 101

Glossary · page 102

Useful Names and Addresses · page 106

Index · page 109

How to Use This Book

Stress and Mental Health is part of a six-volume encyclopedia series of books on health topics significant to junior-high students. These health topics are closely related to each other, and, for this reason, you'll see references to the other volumes in the series appearing throughout the book. You'll also see references to the other pages *within* this book. These references are important because they tell you where you can find more interrelated and interesting information on the specific subject at hand.

Like each of the books in the series, this book is divided into two sections. The first section tells you why it's a good idea for you to know about this health topic and how it affects you. The second section helps you find ways to improve and maintain your health. We include quizzes and plans designed to help you see how these health issues are related to you. It's your responsibility to take advantage of them and apply them to your life. Even though this book was written expressly for you and people your age, you are the one who's in control of learning from it and thereby exercising good health habits for the rest of your life.

PART I:
What's Important For Me To Know About Stress and Mental Health?

When you think of stress, what is the first thing that comes to mind? The way you feel when a parent yells at you? Studying for a biology test? Going on a date?

All these situations play a part in stress. But do you know *why* these situations make you feel nervous? Do you know what happens within your body? Do you know how stress can affect your health?

In this volume, you'll learn the answers to all these questions. Plus, you'll find out how this timely topic applies to your life. Contrary to what you might have been told before, stress doesn't only affect adults.

ENCYCLOPEDIA OF GOOD HEALTH

STRESS AND MENTAL HEALTH

Stress is a natural, necessary life function.

Sometimes we use the word "stress" to describe anything that upsets us: a report card, a fight with a friend, a loud noise. Stress, however, is actually our *reaction* to these things. The situations or objects causing stress are "stressors." Some might call them "hassles," but the two are not completely synonymous. Generally, we try to avoid hassles, but we can't—and don't completely want to—avoid stressors. Try to imagine life without some stress. You wouldn't have any challenges, anything to affect your emotions or anything new or exciting. You wouldn't meet new people, answer questions in class, play a solo in band. Yes, these situations all are stressors, but they also make life interesting and exciting. A life without stressors would mean everything is the same, all the time—and that is boring. Stress, on the other hand, is your body's response to the things that happen around you. It activates you physically and emotionally. It can be as heavy as grief for a dead relative or as light as anxiously waiting for a phone call. And, though stress has been getting a lot of attention lately, it is nothing new; it is a primitive and natural bodily function.

Fight-or-Flight

The story of the caveman is often used to illustrate the fundamentals of stress. It is night, and a prehistoric man sits next to a fire at the opening of his cave. Suddenly from nowhere, a saber-toothed tiger appears in the firelight. The caveman tenses, and automatically, his body reacts, both inwardly and outwardly. He must react in some way in order to survive. He can run, or he can fight, but he can't ponder, or it will be too late. Instead, his body naturally experiences stress and energy, forcing him to either fight off the tiger or flee from it in order to save his life.

ENCYCLOPEDIA OF GOOD HEALTH

STRESS AND MENTAL HEALTH

ENCYCLOPEDIA OF GOOD HEALTH
STRESS AND MENTAL HEALTH

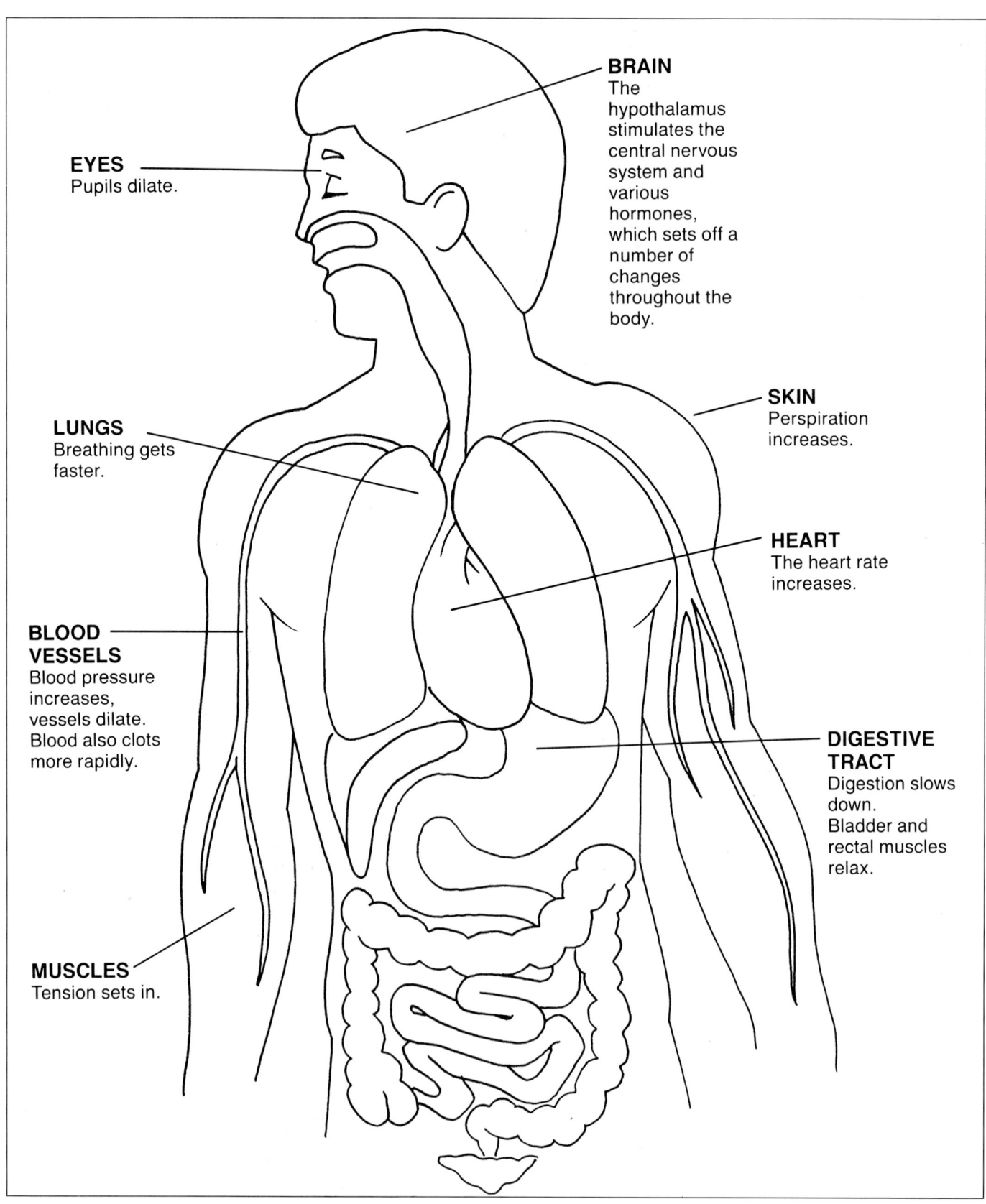

ENCYCLOPEDIA OF GOOD HEALTH
STRESS AND MENTAL HEALTH

Stressors come in all shapes and sizes—from football games to airplane delays. At the same time, stress causes a chain of physical reactions. See below.

What exactly happened to the caveman when he was approached by the tiger? First, he experienced physical changes causing the body to experience stress. The tiger itself wasn't stress; but the *stressor*. Stress was the man's nervous system's reaction to the tiger. His nervous system underwent the following changes:

1. When the man saw and heard the tiger, his eyes and ears instantly sent a message to the brain: "This is a tiger and that means danger." The brain reacted by speeding an "alert!" signal to the hypothalamus, a tiny cluster of nerve cells at the base of the brain. In turn, the hypothalamus set several automatic body functions in motion. Then, specific hormones (body chemicals) helped carry the orders out.

2. Digestion slowed down, too. Before the tiger appeared, most of the caveman's blood was directed to his body's center, aiding the digestion of his last meal (see "Nutrition"). But when he saw the tiger, the blood was instantly diverted to his arms and legs, preparing them for quick action. This helps explain why he might have felt stomach "butterflies" when he first saw the tiger.

3. At the same time, breathing gets faster. The caveman's body rushed more oxygen to the muscles, supplying them for fight or flight (see "Exercise").

4. The heart speeds up, and the blood pressure rises. In anticipation of action, the caveman's body was also speeding blood to the muscles and brain.

5. Nutrients pour from the body's storage system into the bloodstream. Food provides energy, so when the body perceives the need for action, it draws on that energy. The caveman was probably very strong, but this sudden concentration of energy enabled him to run faster or fight harder than he normally would.

6. Muscles tense. When you pictured the caveman in your mind, you probably imagined his body stiffening and tightening up. The blood and oxygen that race to the muscles cause them to react in this way.

7. Perspiration increases. The harder the body works, the more it needs to cool off. Perspiration is the human body's built-in air conditioning system. At the same time, goose bumps form and hair stands on end to improve body cooling.

8. Pupils dilate; eyelids open wider. This helps the stressed individual maximize vision.

9. The blood clots more rapidly. In times of stress, the body actually releases certain blood-clotting chemicals into the bloodstream. If the caveman had been injured by the tiger, his bleeding probably would have stopped sooner than it ordinarily would.

15

ENCYCLOPEDIA OF GOOD HEALTH
STRESS AND MENTAL HEALTH

Recognizing Stressors

Can you differentiate between stress and a stressor? Make sure that you can, because it will help you understand yourself a lot better.

For example, the saber-toothed tiger in the caveman scenario was the stressor. The caveman's physical reaction was stress. However our daily stressors are much different:

- Sherry is running for student council, and the upcoming election has made her very excited. Stressor: The election. Stress: Nervousness, high energy level.
- Scott's parents argue constantly, and he's upset about it. Stressor: Parents' arguments. Stress: Feeling upset.
- Kitty is scared: Today is her first day at a new school. Stressor: The situation of being new. Stress: Feeling scared.

Think of stressful situations that you have experienced. What was the stressor, and what was the resulting stress?

ENCYCLOPEDIA OF GOOD HEALTH

STRESS AND MENTAL HEALTH

other Lifts Car to Save Child

KINGSPORT—A three-year-old girl is listed in good condition at Holston Valley Community Hospital today, after her 140-pound (63-kilogram) mother lifted a 3,000-pound (1350-kilogram) car from the child's pinned legs.

According to police, Megan Searight was playing near her driveway at about 4:00 yesterday afternoon when her parents' parked car rolled and crashed into the Searight home, trapping the toddler beneath the wheels. Cynthia Searight, 29, heard the noise and rushed from the house to her daughter's rescue.

"I simply didn't think," Mrs. Searight said at the hospital this morning. "I did what I had to do. I got the car off her." The child suffered two broken legs, but managed to pull herself from beneath the car.

How does something like this happen? It sounds impossible, but real-life incidents like this have been reported. Doctors explain it as follows: While a person experiences stress, a number of physical changes occur quickly (see page 15). All of them prepare the body for immediate and forceful action. In heavy-stress situations—caused by tremendous stressors like a child in danger—these physical changes can come together to produce a larger-than-life reaction. Under normal circumstances, of course, few people could lift an automobile. But every now and then, we hear about a story as incredible as this.

Do you think of the holidays as a good or bad experience? Either way, they are an example of a stressor. Why? Because holidays involve change: Christmas day is unlike any other day.

17

ENCYCLOPEDIA OF GOOD HEALTH
STRESS AND MENTAL HEALTH

Stress is expensive. In the United States alone, the estimated annual cost caused by work absence and health and insurance charges runs close to $75 billion. The working population missed work over 45 million days in 1985. Total mental health expenditures almost doubled from 1975 to 1984 when Americans spent more than $14 billion.

Modern Stress

Let's update this prehistoric fight-or-flight reaction to a contemporary situation. Walking home after school, you step off a curb to cross the street. Suddenly, you see and hear a car heading straight for you. You jump back onto the sidewalk, saving yourself in the nick of time. What happened in that instant, when you froze in your tracks and realized you were in serious danger?

Once you regain your composure, you realize how hard your heart is beating and how quickly you're breathing. Your forehead or underarms might feel a little damp from perspiration. You might even feel sick to your stomach.

Can you see how similar this is to the situation involving the caveman and the tiger? The stressor was the danger created by the approaching car. Without really thinking about it, you instantly experienced stress, and you reacted. At the same time, your body was experiencing all the changes described on page 15.

Other modern-day stress situations aren't necessarily life-threatening. Unfortunately the body still perceives them to be. Example: You find it difficult to understand your algebra teacher, so you're not doing too well in class, no matter how hard you study. Consequently, when a pop quiz is announced, your body reacts to this stressor. It doesn't matter that the quiz isn't a saber-toothed tiger. Your body braces itself anyway. Your heart beats rapidly; your upper lip is beaded with sweat; your stomach is upset.

You are confronted with a fight-or-flight situation. While you *want* to fly out the door, you know that won't help your grade or reputation. So you do what you have to do: You take the quiz.

This is where stress gets tricky. The caveman released the stress energy his body created by fighting or running from the tiger. It's not so easy for you. Maybe it would be easier if we could avoid people or subjects we don't understand or run away from quizzes, but those aren't always practical solutions. Some stress is necessary, even healthy. But when stress builds with no outlet, health problems occur (see "Prolonged Stress Causes Health Problems," page 43). What's more, life becomes a lot less pleasant. That's why stress is such a recurrent topic, and that's why most of us need to learn how to deal with it.

At the same time, stress isn't always as easy to identify as it was in the caveman story and the algebra quiz story. In the next section, we'll describe other causes of stress.

ENCYCLOPEDIA OF GOOD HEALTH
STRESS AND MENTAL HEALTH

The Good Side of Stress

What would you say if we told you stress is neither good nor bad?

It's true. Stress is a natural, constant part of life, because it involves change, challenge, and emotions. How would you like to suspend this very moment for the rest of your life? That's what a life without any stress would be like, since all events—from birthday parties to ball games—cause some stress. Don't expect your heart to pound every time you walk into a new class; stress differs in intensity and your body will react differently to a horror movie than it will to a real-life mugger. Yet you really can't get through a day without experiencing some sort of stress.

The reason we often hear about stress in a negative light is that many people only associate bad experiences with stress. A blind date may be a good event or a bad event for you, but in either case it's still a stressor.

What determines whether stress is good or bad for you is how you perceive and handle a stressor. A situation that seems extremely stressful to you could leave someone else very calm. Your ability to tolerate a stressor depends on a number of factors: genetics and parental modeling (if your parent handles some stressors well, you may, too); past experiences (events that upset you in the past can instill ongoing fears); your personal attitudes (if you hate smoke, then another person lighting up a cigarette will upset you more than it would irritate someone who chain-smokes); and the number of other stressors in your life (you are coping now, but one more stressor will be one too many).

The following scenario will help you to understand how stress needs to be balanced. Allen is on the first string of his school's basketball team. Naturally, he wants to be "psyched" for the ball games. By getting excited and both mentally and physically preparing himself for the game, he feels he'll play better. In other words, he's using stress to his benefit.

Jeff is a first-string player, too. Yet he reacts to the game differently. He's so nervous he begins to worry about all the mistakes he might make, until the coach finds him crying in the locker room. He is in no condition to play ball. This is letting stress work against you.

The stressor was the same for both boys, but they reacted to it in different ways. Allen had a great game, but it was a bad experience for Jeff. Why? Maybe Jeff had other stressors on his mind, such as a poor report card or an argument with his brother. Or perhaps Jeff is one of those people who doesn't function well with too much stress (see "The Role of Personality," page 39).

The point is this: Stress in itself is not bad. You can take the energy that stress creates and use it to your advantage like Allen did. You should actually welcome some stress, because it makes life exciting. Stress can feel as good as winning a contest or flying in an airplane.

Of course, the frightening, high-impact stressors—such as the death of a friend or moving to a new town—are also things you may encounter. Those stressors don't make you feel good, but you can learn to manage them. First, though, you have to be able to recognize and understand them better. The following pages will help.

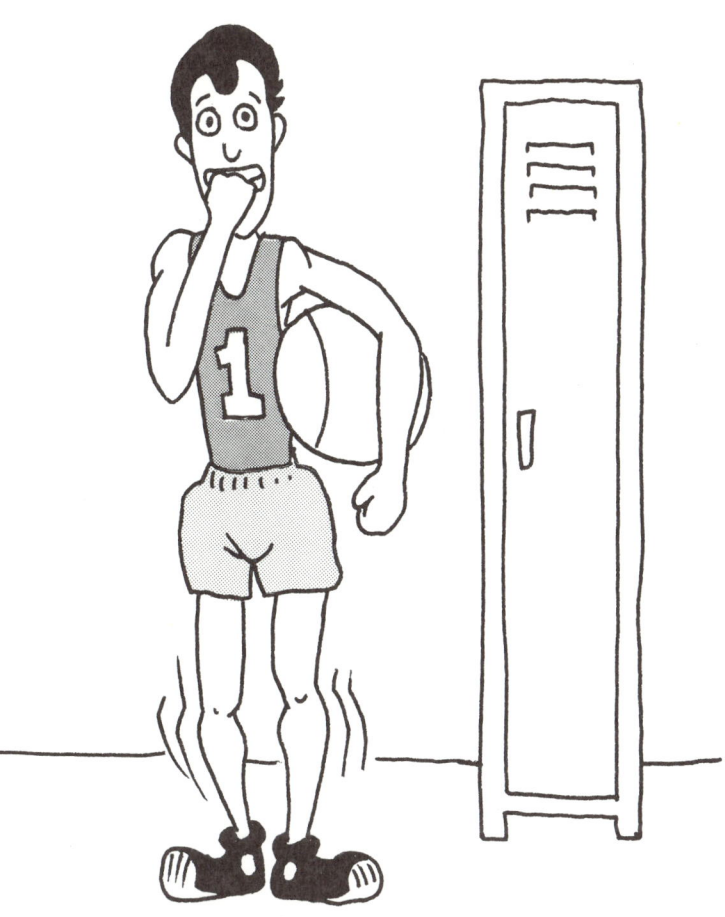

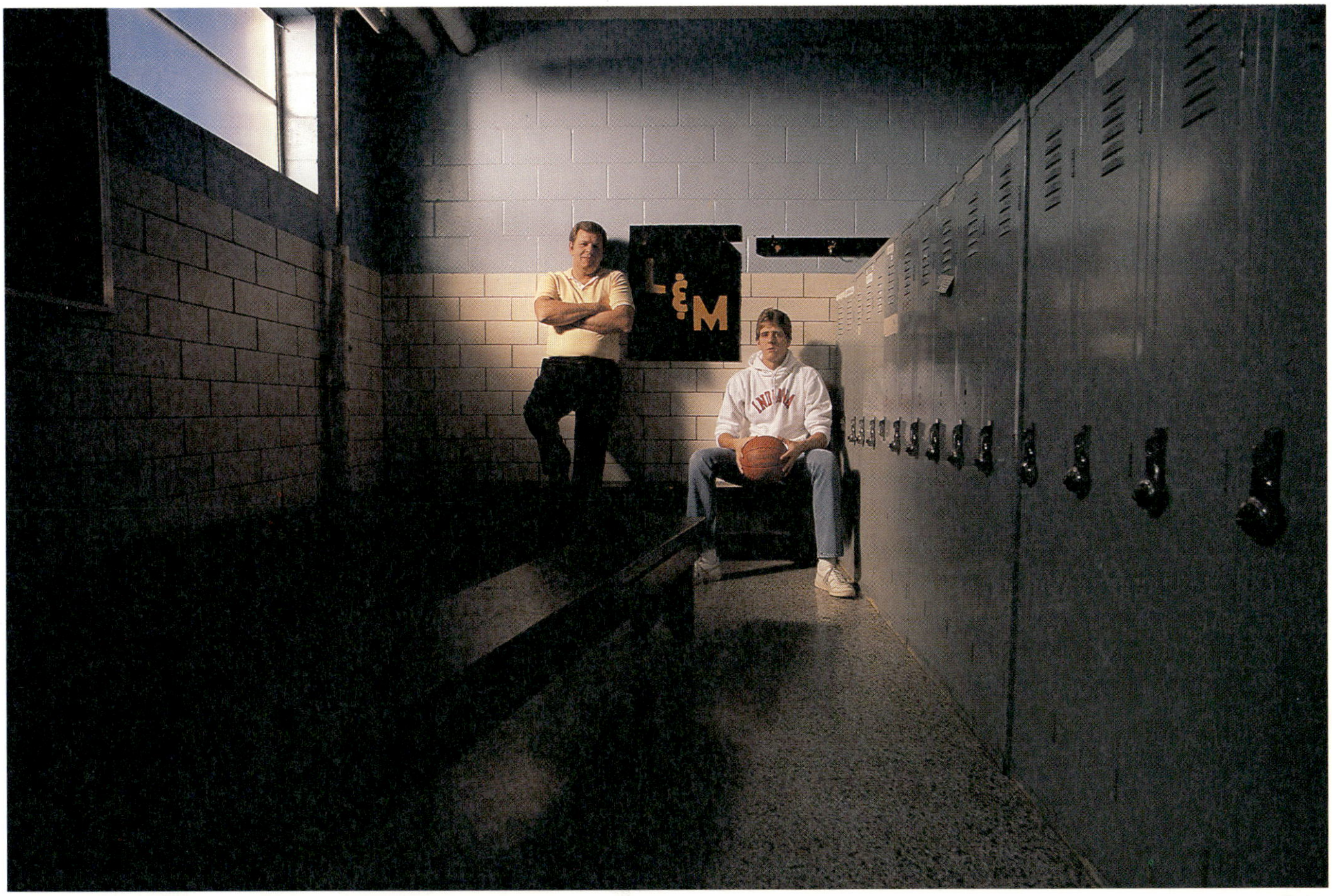

Joe McNally/Wheeler Pictures

ENCYCLOPEDIA OF GOOD HEALTH

STRESS AND MENTAL HEALTH

Stressors come in all shapes, sizes, and forms

In the life of the average junior-high-school student, stressors can be physical or internal, minor or major, and can take place at school or at home. Sometimes they're very apparent. Other times you have to look deeply into the situation to find them. In order to effectively deal with stressors, it is necessary to recognize them.

School

For you, this could be the biggest stressor of all. Consider it safe to say these are some of the best times of your life, but they're also the most challenging. When you advanced from elementary to junior high school, you noticed a difference in schoolwork. Now it's more serious. Classes are more organized, tests are more difficult, and grades are more important. You may not be choosing the subjects that shape your future now, but you will be in high school. Adults sometimes think their problems—paying bills, cleaning the house, managing time—are more stressful, but your schoolwork and decisions demand a lot of you, too.

Other challenges—playing sports, performing in the band, running for student council—are other stressors you face at school. These challenges make school fun, but competition and hard work can be very stressful.

Friends

Getting a good grade on a paper is one thing. Becoming popular with your peers is another. Someday, popularity will probably mean less to you. But if you're like many junior-high-school students, it's close to the top of your stressor list now. You want close friends you can confide in. You want to be well liked. Maybe you wish you could be recognized as a cheerleader, student council president, or basketball star.

Sometimes you may make these stressors into bigger problems than they should be—that is, blow them out of proportion. Yet, they are important to you right now (see "Self-Made Stressors," page 24). It's undeniable that such triggers can contribute to your overall stress level.

ENCYCLOPEDIA OF GOOD HEALTH
STRESS AND MENTAL HEALTH

30 THINGS YOU MAY NOT HAVE THOUGHT ARE STRESSFUL

1. Going to the dentist
2. Kissing someone for the first time
3. Giving a speech
4. Meeting your mom's new boyfriend (or your dad's new girlfriend)
5. Waiting for an important phone call
6. Hearing that a friend was in a car accident
7. Getting asked to the Prom
8. *Not* getting asked to the Prom
9. Shooting a foul shot
10. Driving a car
11. Getting sick
12. Making straight A's
13. Failing a test
14. Fighting with your kid brother [roommate]
15. Opening birthday gifts [a condom]
16. Choosing a very special birthday [christmas] gift
17. Being afraid
18. Saying "no" to a cigarette or alcohol
19. Apologizing to a teacher [proffessor]
20. Missing the bus [a class]
21. Graduating from junior high [college]
22. Winning first place—or coming in last place
23. Making your parent cry
24. Staying up too late at night
25. Getting laughed at
26. Representing your school at an all-star game, meeting, or contest
27. Seeing your ex-girl/boyfriend with someone else
28. Riding a roller coaster
29. Losing a pet
30. Going to school

23

ENCYCLOPEDIA OF GOOD HEALTH
STRESS AND MENTAL HEALTH

Self-Made Stressors

A. Scarlett has had it with her brother. He insists on playing his cassette tapes at maximum volume when he knows she's trying to nap.

B. Brooks wants very much to make first-chair trumpet. He has already decided that if he doesn't make it, he'll be devastated.

Which of these people has a case of self-made stress? Obviously, Brooks does. Scarlett has a stressor that is a problem, but it's not of her own doing. As for Brooks' situation, the trumpet tryout itself could be considered a stressor. But most of the stress Brooks is feeling is the result of his own thoughts.

Once again, your interpretation of a stressor makes all the difference in its impact. A stressor doesn't affect you all by itself. You have to *see* it as a stressor first.

In Scarlett's situation, if she wanted to hear her brother's music she probably wouldn't perceive the loud music as a stressor. Similarly, if Brooks had less interest in the trumpet audition, it wouldn't be a stressor. Unlike the saber-toothed tiger, most activities today become stressors if you think of them as stressors. That is, these stressful situations are self-made because they involve an element of interpretation. However, it's easy to see that some situations can be made much more stressful than they need to be. You'll be seeing other examples of self-made stress throughout these pages, but here are a few others to give you an idea of what one is. In each of these cases, most of the stress is in your own thoughts.

- Your boyfriend, Jeff, didn't call tonight, and he always does on Tuesdays. You believe that he is calling another girl and is going to break up with you tomorrow. Now you feel you're falling apart.
- Gwen said something strange about your new shoes this morning. For the rest of the day, you worried about what was wrong with them and what other people were saying.
- You recently saw a movie about a nuclear bomb. The more you think about it, the more you're afraid a nuclear war is on the way.

  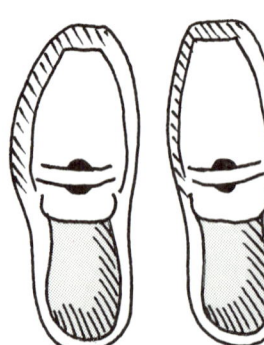

24

Boyfriends and Girlfriends

Pounding heart, sweaty palms, heavy breathing—when these physical changes occur, it's often when you're talking to a member of the opposite sex. It's stressful enough when you're just trying to get noticed by someone you like. Once you've established a relationship, however, other stressors come into play. You may sometimes be angry with your boyfriend or girlfriend and have mixed feelings of jealousy and insecurity. In such situations, you probably feel your blood pressure rise.

Self-made stressors can be a problem, too (see page 24). For example, if your boyfriend or girlfriend tries to persuade you to change something about yourself that you don't feel any need to change, that person is acting as a stressor. If you begin to worry that he or she will leave you if you don't change, and do something you don't want to do, then you are producing self-made stress by letting the stressor exert control over you.

ENCYCLOPEDIA OF GOOD HEALTH
STRESS AND MENTAL HEALTH

For you, a stressor might be an argument with your coach. For parents, it could be a long day at the office.

Family

Mom wants you to get a job after school. Your younger brother, Sammy, wants you to play with him. Your older brother, Joel, ignores you. And Dad, who's going through his own crisis, is hardly ever home.

These are just a few examples of how family can act as a stressor. It's not only a question of demands and pressures from other family members, your concern for others (you worry about where Dad is all the time), obligations (Mom doesn't ask you to look after Sammy, but you know you should), and relationship problems (you know Joel loves you, but you never quite got along) can also add up.

Of course families can be the source of positive stressors, too: vacations, the birth of a new sister, and holiday dinners are all positive situations.

What stressful situations develop in your family?

26

ENCYCLOPEDIA OF GOOD HEALTH

STRESS AND MENTAL HEALTH

Emotional Stressors

In self-made stress and the other stressors explained here, you can see how big a role emotions play. Fear, anxiety, impatience, and depression can produce the same physical stress reaction as a saber-toothed tiger can; the brain interprets the situation as stress and prepares the body for action—even if the action never takes place. If you are constantly afraid of making a bad grade, for example, your fear can put you in a state of stress.

What's more, an existing emotion can make any stressor seem more stressful. Here's how:

- Anyone would feel some stress at having to write a term paper over the weekend. But for Duane, who has been depressed since his grandfather died, the paper is even more upsetting.
- Remember Jeff (page 20), who worked himself into a frenzy over the basketball game? A certain amount of anxiety would help him get excited about the game, but too much caused a highly stressful situation. One reason the anxiety proved to be too much: He was already upset over a bad practice session.
- Shannon experiences a great deal of stress whenever she rides in a car. The reason: She was involved in a serious car accident as a little girl, and she's afraid it will happen again.

Friends and peers will always figure in your life as a source of stress. As a junior-high student, you're probably beginning to notice this. Suddenly, popularity is more important than ever.

ENCYCLOPEDIA OF GOOD HEALTH

STRESS AND MENTAL HEALTH

hort-Term and Long-Term Stressors

Here's something else you've probably noticed in reading about all these different stressors: Some are temporary situations that go away almost as soon as they appear. Others seem to build up; they don't occupy your every waking moment, but they're always there.

Let's look at the caveman again: His problems were over when he escaped from the saber-toothed tiger. All the physical changes he experienced disappeared once he had a chance to sit down, wipe his forehead, and catch his breath. A present-day example: You fly off the handle when a friend teases you. You're so mad you want to shove him into his locker and leave him there. Once he apologizes and you realize he was only joking, however, you calm down. It was a stressful situation for a moment there, but now it's all over.

Generally, short-term stressors cause fewer problems than long-term stressors. Your body reacts, then returns to normal. It's the long-lasting stressors we're most concerned about. The stress signals don't let up, and the body suffers (see "Prolonged Stress Causes Health Problems," page 43). An example of a long-term stressor could be a parent's problem with alcohol. The fact that you see Mom in a bad situation night after night may not be life threatening, yet your emotions about the situation cause the same "fight-or-flight" stress signals (see "Substance Abuse").

Another long-term stressor could be a weight problem. If extra weight causes more than a few problems (pressure from your folks, physical limitations at school), your body may experience a constant state of stress. This can result in many health problems, which you'll learn about later (see "Nutrition").

ENCYCLOPEDIA OF GOOD HEALTH

STRESS AND MENTAL HEALTH

Daily Problems

The alarm clock sends you scrambling for the off switch, but you fall back into bed before making it to your feet. The next thing you know, Dad is pulling you out of bed—you're running late. You find your way to the shower and get blasted with a shock of ice-cold water; you have little time to get dressed and eat breakfast; and you have to run all the way to school. A teacher stops you in the hall, asks why you're not in class, then slaps you with an after-school punishment. Once you make it to typing class, you're told you missed a quiz—and you won't be allowed to make it up....

One piece of burnt toast or one remark from a parent won't always send your stress level soaring. But taken together, daily problems can be very stressing—not life threatening, but taxing nonetheless. Of course, a little stress management works wonders in these matters. We'll address that in Part II.

Big Changes

Moving from seventh grade to eight grade—never mind moving to a new town—is a change. Making a new friend is a change. Many stressors center on a change. If we don't have *enough* of these changes, we may feel bored and purposeless.

Then there are the monumental changes in life, the ones that rate highest in scientists' measurements of stressors (see "How High Is Your Stress Level?" page 36). While they're sometimes impossible to avoid, people have the most trouble adjusting to them. Stressors resulting from big changes contribute to overwhelming stress.

These kinds of changes involve the serious illness or death of a close relative, a new brother or sister, moving to a different town, parental divorce—and anything else that alters something important in your life. These stressors don't always have a negative impact, but because they change one's life, they have to be managed with care. You'll find out how later.

Environment

Pollution, crowding, noise, violence, and other "outside" sources of stress also take their toll on you. In fact, people in big cities, where these things are a way of life, are known to have a higher level of stress compared to small-town dwellers.

Environmental stressors vary but produce the same effects. A jackhammer running outside your window while you're trying to study, being packed into a subway, or witnessing the mugging of an elderly lady are all stressors that we can't always control, so it's important to learn how to manage them.

Physical Stressors

Let's say you stay up until 4:00 a.m. studying for a test. The next day you're tired, which adds to the stress you feel because of the test. Neglecting your nutritional needs can also lead to stress. Without necessary nutrients your body can't operate in peak condition, and as a result you put a strain on yourself and increase the impact of everyday stressors like tests, ball games, and recitals (see "Nutrition").

Injuries and illnesses act as stressors, too. Remember the way you felt last time you had a bad cold? Not only did your throat and head hurt, you also felt bad psychologically—your spirits were low. As anyone who's been hurt in an accident can tell you, injuries cause stress, too. Not only is the body experiencing stress as it heals, the victim also has to deal with other changes: recovery, disrupted schedules, lack of exercise, and so on.

Of course, people who suffer from chronic diseases (diabetes, heart disease) or pain (arthritis, migraine headaches) have to deal with a different type of stress—one that doesn't go away. The emotional impact of being handicapped or disabled is even greater.

ENCYCLOPEDIA OF GOOD HEALTH
STRESS AND MENTAL HEALTH

Clearly, life in large cities—such as New York—can be more stressful than living in a small town. While there were nearly 9,000 crimes committed for every 100,000 people living in large cities (population over 250,000), there were about half that number committed in relatively small towns (population 10,000 to 25,000). In rural areas, the rate drops to about 2,000 crimes for every 100,000 people. However, in sparsely populated areas there are other forms of stress, such as isolation, unemployment, and lack-of-people pressure.

ENCYCLOPEDIA OF GOOD HEALTH
STRESS AND MENTAL HEALTH

eople Pressure

- Penny is Laurie's good friend. Unfortunately, Penny has a drug problem, and because Laurie cares about her, Penny's problem is Laurie's stressor. What's more, Penny pressures Laurie into taking drugs with her.
- As the school's first-string quarterback, Bruce has a very promising year ahead of him. The coach is excited about Bruce's potential, so he pushes him a little harder than the rest of the team. The whole team is counting on him for a championship season.
- Mike comes from an outstanding family: His parents often talk about their very successful school years, and his sister followed in their footsteps. Mike has always been a good student, but he knows even more is expected of him. His parents might not *say* he should be making straight A's, but they're always asking him if he's trying hard enough.

It's nice to have support from friends, family, and teachers. Naturally, we want to please everyone and to be the best friend, daughter, or student possible. We even welcome the stress that people provide for us. An enthusiastic coach makes us try harder; the needs of a friend make us feel important.

Beyond a certain point, however, other people's encouragement, demands, problems, and our own personal effort to succeed cause us to reach an uncomfortable stress level. At this point in your life, you may get pressure from a lot of people, which in turn, makes you put a lot of pressure on yourself.

You're smart enough to know that too much pressure from people will make you depressed—even if this pressure is meant to help you. It pays to be able to recognize this stressor and know how to handle it.

The more time you spend with other people, the more important it is to find time for yourself. However, isolation can be just as stressful as a lack of "private time."

ENCYCLOPEDIA OF GOOD HEALTH
STRESS AND MENTAL HEALTH

Lack-of-People Pressure

People pressure is one thing. Isolation from others is another. In fact, studies show that individuals with the fewest social contacts experience higher stress levels than people with many acquaintances. The result: emotional problems, accidents, physical ailments, disease, and even death. In other words, if you were on a deserted island, you would be more stressed than if you were among people.

The reason why social isolation affects people negatively is probably related to the buffering effect of a social support system. We know that having people to talk to, to test our thoughts and feelings on, and to get support from helps us deal with stress. This is one of the management musts you'll learn in Part II.

33

ENCYCLOPEDIA OF GOOD HEALTH

STRESS AND MENTAL HEALTH

eople Pressure: Are You A Victim?

Answer yes or no to the following questions.

1. Think about your goals. Did you set them for yourself or because someone else wanted you to?
2. Do you often find yourself doing things you really don't want to do, but you do them because someone expects you to?
3. Do you have trouble differentiating between what *you* like and what people near you like?
4. Is it hard for you to say "no" to others?
5. Do you feel like you never have time to think about yourself?

If you said yes to any of these questions, you might have a case of people pressure. You can't cure it overnight. Start by doing one thing such as saying "no" to someone, explaining to Dad that you don't *want* to be the smartest kid in school, or just try putting yourself first in your thoughts for a change. Of course, a little bit of people pressure is natural, even healthy. But don't let it back you into an uncomfortable corner.

ENCYCLOPEDIA OF GOOD HEALTH
STRESS AND MENTAL HEALTH

Chemical Stressors

When we say "chemical stressors," what do you think of? Pollution in the air? Pesticides in our water?

If so, you're partially on target. As you know, stress involves several physical body changes (see page 15). Since stress is a very natural part of life, we are equipped to handle it to a certain extent. When you don't have enough stress, you get bored; when you get too much, the body sends out danger signals.

This delicate balance—as much physical as it is mental—can be thrown off by body-altering chemicals. No, it isn't always obvious; we usually can't even tell. Yet chemicals around us—everything from nail polish remover to car exhaust—can subtly contribute to stress. So can chemicals we ingest:

- Caffeine and other stimulants in coffee, tea, and soft drinks increase the output of stress hormones.
- A high-sugar diet can lead to fluctuating blood sugar, a cause of fatigue and irritability.
- Nicotine in cigarettes directly stimulates the adrenal gland, an organ that produces stress hormones.
- Alcohol in excess damages the digestive and cardiovascular (heart and blood) systems, and any physical problems or illness (see page 30) contributes to stress. Drinking alcohol not only produces physical stress, but may also result in added complications, such as disapproving relatives and missed appointments.
- Drugs are chemicals designed to achieve certain effects in the body. Doctors know how to use these drugs without disturbing or damaging our bodies' delicate systems. Taken without this guidance, drugs are among the most dangerous stressors. Like alcohol, these substances create stress within you *and* create stressful situations.

Oddly enough, people rely on some of these chemicals to *relieve* stress. Temporarily, cigarettes, alcohol, marijuana and drugs, especially tranquilizers may help stressed individuals feel better. In the long run, however, you can see how chemicals only create more stress by producing damaging physical and emotional side effects and, therefore, more stressful problems such as an inability to deal with life's demands. Therefore, using them really doesn't make sense (see "Nutrition" and "Substance Abuse").

Other Stressors

School, friends, family, and major life changes—these are probably the stressors that affect you the most these days. It's impossible for us to list them all, but after reading the preceding pages, you can probably recognize a stressor in your own life.

As you get older, your stressor list will shift: Money, work, politics, and a host of other topics will occupy your thoughts. While these "adult stressors" may seem more important, the challenges you face today are just as stressful. It's smart, then, to learn how to deal with them *now*. This way, you'll be more prepared for the future. Additionally, you'll enjoy the present a lot more by being able to deal with your problems more effectively.

QUIZ: HOW HIGH IS YOUR STRESS LEVEL?

A move to a new town would probably be a heavier stressor for you than for your preschool brother. On the other hand, vacation is probably a bigger deal for your parents than it is to you, since they have to do most of the planning, packing—and paying.

As you can see, stressors are different for everyone. The chart below rates the events most significant to *you*. It's adapted from The Social Readjustment Ratings Scale, devised by American doctors T.H. Holmes and R.H. Rahe. You can determine your personal stress score by adding up the number of points next to the events you have experienced during the past twelve months. Add the numbers up on a separate piece of paper.

Death of a parent	100
Death of a close friend	73
Death of a close family member	73
Becoming pregnant or getting someone pregnant	65
Divorce between parents	65
Going to jail or reform school	63
Getting caught using drugs	60
Beginning to use drugs	55
Failing a whole year of school	50
Personal major illness or injury	50
Change in health of family member	44
Getting expelled or suspended	42
Pressure to take drugs	39
New baby brother or sister	39
Troubles with parents	39
Moving to a different school or town	38
New girlfriend or boyfriend	38
Increased work load at school	38
Outstanding personal achievement or award	36
Pressure to have sex	36
Bad report card	35
Argument with teacher	35
Argument with brother, sister, or friend	35
Breaking up with boyfriend or girlfriend	35
Driver's license test	34
First date	34
Braces	33
Change in sleeping habits	29
Making a team (sports, debate, etc.)	28
First day of school	26
Big change in eating or exercise habits	15
Vacation	13
Christmas	12

ENCYCLOPEDIA OF GOOD HEALTH

STRESS AND MENTAL HEALTH

SCORING

300 and higher: You've had a very stressful year. No doubt some of this stress you still carry with you. Turn to Part II for some help in managing stress. People with scores of 300 or more are at the highest health risk.

150–299: According to the stress points you've accumulated during the past year, you are one-third *less* likely to develop a health problem than people who score over 300. Be sure to follow all the stress-handling tips in Part II.

Below 150: Chances are you have a low risk of developing stress-related health problems, but read ahead for pointers on how to stay healthy.

Imprisonment would be a source of stress for anyone. Imagine how much stress people experience when they serve even a few hours for drunk driving.

ENCYCLOPEDIA OF GOOD HEALTH
STRESS AND MENTAL HEALTH

Is this guy nervous? What about the girl? If she feels her heart beating faster, and his hands feel sweaty, they're both experiencing symptoms of stress.

ENCYCLOPEDIA OF GOOD HEALTH

STRESS AND MENTAL HEALTH

The Role of Personality

What kind of personality is more prone to stress?

A. Impatient, aggressive, competitive, ambitious, and hardworking

B. Calm, relaxed, and less ambitious

If you picked A, you're correct. Psychologists believe there are two important personality types related to stress: A's and B's. The Type A's set high goals and demands of themselves and others. The Type B's are exactly the opposite, and consequently, are at less risk for stress and its health problems.

Which category do you fall in? Few of us have all the characteristics of either type. You probably possess traits of both personalities, but you lean toward one more than the other.

You should understand how much your personality can influence the way you respond to stress. For example, if you don't have a very good opinion of yourself, talking to a person you just met could be more stressful than if you were more confident. Recognizing these personality traits gives you more insight into stressful situations.

Ways to combat loneliness: Call or visit a close friend, join a club or get a pet, go to an art gallery, concert, or other people-oriented gathering.

39

ENCYCLOPEDIA OF GOOD HEALTH
STRESS AND MENTAL HEALTH

Stress Test

Do you know someone who seems to thrive on high-stress situations? Who can't say "no" to any challenge—even if it means as much work as he can handle? Who doesn't feel really good about himself unless he's in the middle of a difficult situation?

People who fit these descriptions are typically Type A's. You might say they're "hooked" on constant challenges. To pull them away from all their stressors would be even more stressful than the stressors themselves. Consequently, these people are usually the most outstanding, productive individuals. Does this describe you in any way?

The bad news is that if an over-achiever or perfectionist does not have the skills to handle the challenge, he runs the highest risk of health damage through his response to stress. If a person does have the organizational skills to handle challenges then the continuous demands will probably get to him (see "Organizing Smarts," page 73). The good news is you can learn how far you can push yourself without making yourself sick. It's not that you should want to change your personality; you should just know when—and how—to slow down.

ENCYCLOPEDIA OF GOOD HEALTH

STRESS AND MENTAL HEALTH

Where there's a lot of people and commotion, there's usually a lot of stress. Not that these workers at the New York Stock Exchange (opposite page) are feeling bad stress. Not only do they thrive on the excitement, but it can also help their job performance. (Above) Winning is stressful. Don't believe it? Think back to the last time you did something great. Didn't you feel excited, full of nervous energy?

ENCYCLOPEDIA OF GOOD HEALTH
STRESS AND MENTAL HEALTH

Prolonged Stress Causes Health Problems

We've already explained that stress is perfectly normal, even necessary. Nevertheless, the body strives to maintain a stable psychological state. That is, it knows how to handle the ups and downs of stress, but the minute a stressor approaches, the body reacts.

A theory by biologist Hans Selye explains this process. The first stage is *alarm*. Basically, this is the same thing as the fight-or-flight response, in which the stressor signals the brain and all the physical changes take place (see page 15).

Stage two is *resistance*, when the body begins to return to normal. It demands a great deal of energy, but the stress symptoms diminish and disappear.

These first two stages are to be expected in most stressful situations. The third stage, however, occurs when stress does not diminish or disappear. When *exhaustion* sets in, the body tires of resisting stress and runs out of energy. At this point, even a small amount of additional stress can cause big problems.

Stress Signals

When your resistance resources are overworked, your exhausted body stops functioning smoothly. The signs may show up physically, psychologically, or behaviorally. What's more, they affect each other, causing you to fall into a vicious cycle. Example: If stress disrupts your sleep, the lack of rest may upset you even more. After all, you have to sleep in order to do well at school. Unfortunately, worrying about lack-of-sleep increases stress even more, until psychologically, you're depressed, and behaviorally, you cry a lot.

Considering how stress arouses the physical fight-or-flight reaction, it's easy to see that prolonged stress would produce *physical* symptoms. Because digestion is affected, for example, ulcers (stomach sores caused by digestive acids) can develop. Other organs can also become targets, or symptoms may arise in different combinations. Before serious illnesses develop, however, you'll probably see some other signals that appear frequently and be able to avoid them.

Physical Signs

- Back pain
- Constipation
- Diarrhea
- Dizziness
- Dry mouth
- Excess perspiration
- Excessive hunger
- Exhaustion
- Fainting
- Headaches
- Heartburn
- Insomnia
- Muscle spasms
- Nausea
- No appetite
- Pounding heart
- Shortness of breath
- Skin rashes
- Trembling hands
- Upset stomach

ENCYCLOPEDIA OF GOOD HEALTH
STRESS AND MENTAL HEALTH

Emotions, as you know, play a big part in stress. Not only can anxiety, depression, irritability, fear, guilt, and boredom cause stress, but they can also be *psychological* signs of stress. If your parents' divorce has you uptight, for example, you might react with anger. Your clue to the fact that you're overloaded with stress could be that you are constantly upset and disagreeable, which affects your schoolwork, your relationships with friends, your performance in athletics, music, art, drama, and so on.

Here is another example of psychological stress signs. Let's say you are very active as an officer of the pep club and 4-H club, member of the yearbook staff and girl's basketball team, and president of your church's youth group. And of course, there's always homework. Most likely you're beginning to feel overstressed. You feel frustrated and cry without being sure why. You may also snap and yell at people. In this situation listen to your emotions, they are trying to tell you something. As you can see, psychological symptoms only complicate things because they cause additional stress.

Psychological Signs

- Anger
- Anxiety
- Apathy
- Boredom
- Depression
- Fatigue
- Fear of death
- Frustration
- Guilt
- Hopelessness
- Hostility
- Impatience
- Inability to concentrate
- Irritability
- Rejection
- Restlessness

ENCYCLOPEDIA OF GOOD HEALTH

STRESS AND MENTAL HEALTH

Like all athletes, these guys are feeling excited, nervous, and tense before the ballgame. This kind of stress can make or break you. See page 20.

ENCYCLOPEDIA OF GOOD HEALTH
STRESS AND MENTAL HEALTH

Right this moment, you can probably think of someone who plays with their hair. Next time you notice it, ask why they're uptight.

When your body comes across a stressor, it prepares itself for a high-energy fight-or-flight response. However, this energy doesn't always get used. When too much pent-up energy is created, it makes itself known in all kinds of *behavioral* signs.

Any behavior that isn't typical could be a symptom of stress: talking too fast or too loud, pulling at hair, foot-tapping, grinding the teeth, and so on. No doubt you're familiar with these signs. Most of us have a friend who is a fingernail-biter or a brother who's suddenly accident-prone. If behavior changes are unlike a person, they may be a tip-off to problems. It doesn't necessarily count if someone has always been a fingernail-biter. To release pent-up stress, doctors recommend physical activity which unleashes some of the energy your body creates during stress. More information on this is on page 82 ("The Go-With-It-Solution") and in "Exercise."

Behavioral Signs

- Biting lips
- Foot-tapping or -turning
- Grinding teeth
- Impulsive actions
- Moving in tense, jerky ways
- Nervous tics
- Overreacting
- Stuttering
- Swearing
- Touching hair, ears, or nose

ENCYCLOPEDIA OF GOOD HEALTH

STRESS AND MENTAL HEALTH

Bad Habits Get Worse

Sometimes people turn to alcohol, smoking, or drugs to help them relieve stress (see "Chemical Stressors," page 35). For whatever reasons people depend on these substances, a change in use can be another sign of stress.

Let's say Dad has an occasional beer after work. However, when a lot of people begin to be laid off at his job, he becomes upset. Instead of drinking one beer a night he drinks two, then three, then he finishes off a six-pack.

One way to look at this is to realize that Dad was trying to relax. The other side of the coin is that he was reacting to increased stress. Instead of pulling at his hair or tapping his toes, his nervous energy caused him to keep putting a can to his lips. For the moment, the beer *did* relax Dad, since alcohol, a depressant, slows down the body and shuts down the mind (see "Chemical Stressors," page 35, and "Substance Abuse").

The same thing happens with cigarette smokers: They panic over a deadline and keep reaching for cigarettes to chemically alter their mood. Drug habits—from sleeping pills to cocaine—can also worsen during stressful periods.

Smoking cigarettes puts people in a catch-22 situation. Smokers often turn to cigarettes to help relieve stress, but cigarettes actually release stress-inducing nicotine into the bloodstream. (See "Substance Abuse.")

ENCYCLOPEDIA OF GOOD HEALTH

STRESS AND MENTAL HEALTH

QUIZ: LIFE SIGNS

We have talked about physical, psychological, and behavioral stress signals, and you should now be able to recognize them in yourself. On your own piece of paper, draw three columns. Read the statements below, and every time one seems to apply to you, write in the italicized word under the appropriate column. Your paper should look something like this:

Physical	**Psychological**	**Behavioral**
Headaches	Irritable	Stuttering

PHYSICAL

1. I get frequent *headaches.*
2. I often feel queasy or nauseous; I have an *upset stomach.*
3. My back hurts, but it's not because I strained it by lifting something or overexercising. It's more of a tension *backache.*
4. I don't get *skin rashes* from poison ivy or from the sun; they just appear for no obvious reason.
5. I feel *exhausted* all the time—even when I get plenty of rest.
6. I often have *muscle aches,* but I don't know why. I haven't been doing any new exercises or unusual activity lately.
7. I seem to have *frequent colds.*
8. I expect my heart to beat faster when a teacher calls on me or I have to shoot a foul shot. But I seem to have a *pounding heart* at unusual times.
9. I've had a recent *change in appetite;* I'm hungry all the time (or, I never seem to be hungry).
10. I get *heartburn* a lot, and I don't think it is a result of what I've been eating.
11. When I get nervous, I get *diarrhea*—and that's been happening a lot lately.
12. I have a problem with *constipation.*
13. I have trouble falling asleep *(insomnia).*
14. Even when I'm not doing anything particularly strenuous, I sweat a lot *(excess perspiration).*
15. My hands have been *trembling.*
16. I've been experiencing *dryness of mouth.*
17. I've been having *dizzy* and/or *fainting spells.*
18. At unusual times, I've had *shortness of breath.*

PSYCHOLOGICAL

19. I'm more and more *restless;* I can't seem to be content with one thing for very long.
20. I feel so *hopeless,* like there's no sense in believing in or working for anything. It doesn't seem as if things are going to get any better.
21. I feel *hostile,* like I want to lash out and hurt people all the time.
22. I am *impatient* with everything; I don't like to wait. I want to get on with things.
23. I am very *irritable;* little things upset me and aggravate me.
24. I feel *anxious,* like something is about to happen but I don't know what. I can't relax.
25. I feel I'm constantly *angry*—always mad at the world.
26. I'm *apathetic;* I can't seem to care about things, even important things. They just don't matter. Nothing matters.
27. I'm *bored*—not just bored after school or bored in class, but always bored.
28. I've been *depressed* a lot. I can't seem to be happy.
29. I *fear* becoming injured or failing at something so much that it's interfering with my life.
30. No matter what I do, I can't seem to get rid of a sense of *guilt.* It's always with me.
31. I feel *rejected,* like no one wants me or loves me.
32. *Shame* is my problem; I feel disgusted with myself and/or my situation.
33. I *distrust* people on principle; I always think they're up to something, something that will work to my disadvantage.
34. Lately, I've had very *poor concentration.*
35. I am more and more *forgetful.*
36. I have unexplained *mood swings;* one minute I'm up, the next I'm down. These are more drastic than they've ever been.

Behavior is a big giveaway for signs of tension. An occasional outburst of anger or tears is normal, but when it happens frequently over a long period of time, it may indicate serious stress-related problems.

ENCYCLOPEDIA OF GOOD HEALTH

STRESS AND MENTAL HEALTH

One way to help you handle stress: Seek support from friends. For more information, see page 89.

BEHAVIORAL

37. I can't stop *touching* my hair, ears, nose (or other body parts).
38. *Biting my lips* is becoming a more frequent habit.
39. I've been *tapping my feet* more than usual.
40. I find myself *swearing* at little things.
41. For reasons I can't explain, I seem to do things quickly, without thinking *(impulsive actions)*.
42. I recently noticed that I've been *grinding my teeth*.
43. I've never stuttered much before, but I'm *stuttering* now.
44. I *talk or laugh differently;* my speech is faster or my laughter is higher-pitched and nervous.
45. I find myself *moving in tense, jerky ways*.
46. I've been pulling away from family and friends, *limiting my social contact*.
47. I've been *biting my nails* quite a bit lately.
48. Lately, I've experienced other unusual behavior patterns (write them down).

ENCYCLOPEDIA OF GOOD HEALTH

STRESS AND MENTAL HEALTH

ENCYCLOPEDIA OF GOOD HEALTH

STRESS AND MENTAL HEALTH

Psychologists believe that involvement with pets is good therapy for certain individuals. A recent study conducted with elderly people in nursing homes showed they were healthier and happier when animals were brought to them for regular visits.

EXPLANATION

Look at your lists of signs. You probably have a good collection. Chances are, all of these aren't stress symptoms. Study each of them and ask yourself these questions:

1. Have I noticed this sign lately? Is this the way I've always been?
2. Have other people noticed this change in me? Have they expressed concern?
3. Is stress the only possible explanation for this sign?
4. Think back to times when you know you experienced stress. Did you notice this sign then?

If you answered "no" to these questions for any of the signs you listed, you may erase the sign. If you answered "yes" for any of the signs you wrote down, you should leave those on your list. Obviously, there is no right or wrong answer here, so if you're sure that one of the listed signs is a stress symptom, you should not erase it. Use your best judgement for this test.

Now, take a close look at the listed stress signs. Can you pinpoint the stressors that might be causing these signs? Write down the possibilities, as you might a math problem. By studying these stress signals and potential stressors, you'll be able to visualize the problems and answers. (Save your lists of symptoms and possible stressors for Part II, where you'll map out stress *solutions*.)

Note: If any of these signs are threatening to your health (skin rashes, fainting spells, etc.), it's best to see a doctor.

Breakdowns

Once the body begins to give you physical, psychological, and behavioral signs, it's time to do something about stress. If these signs are ignored, chances are something even more serious will develop.

For one, the stress signs described above could get worse: backaches become unbearable, exhaustion confines you to bed, emotional outbursts are more frequent. Other stress signs may appear in addition to previous ones. Or all these warnings could turn into one big problem.

Physical Illnesses and Disorders

In some cases, stress directly affects parts of our bodies until illnesses or disorders develop. Because the fight-or-flight reaction slows the digestive process, ulcers and colitis (inflammation of a part of the large intestine) can develop—in addition to chronic diarrhea, constipation, nausea, heartburn, and indigestion.

The respiratory (breathing) system is affected by the stress reaction, too. So prolonged stress can aggravate asthma, increase the number of colds and respiratory infections you catch, and cause hyperventilation (breathing too fast and too deep). Among the most serious stress-related health problems, of course, are high blood pressure and heart disease. Studies have shown that Type A people are at higher risk for heart attacks. When they "calmed" their hard-working, overaggressive behavior, however, they reduced their risk.

It's easy to see how stress causes high blood pressure, which can lead to heart disease. During the stress reaction, the heart beats faster and blood pressure rises in order to move energy to the muscles. This is a natural function, but can create problems when the body is subjected to constant stress.

Other health problems may be linked to a breakdown of the body's immune system. Doctors have proposed the theory that when the stress level in the body stays too high for too long, it wears down the network of organs, tissues, and white blood cells that fight against disease. Without this important system, none of us could survive; we would be defenseless against the billions of germs and viruses out there. When stress causes the immune system to break down, the body is less able to deal with stress. Therefore, diseases have a chance to invade the body.

To a certain extent, an immune system breakdown could bring about a number of diseases, even those not caused by germs and viruses. Some recent research suggests that a high-stress lifestyle also increases the risk of developing cancer. When the immune system isn't working properly, the disease possibilities run the gamut, from diabetes to tuberculosis.

Can Stress Make You Sick?

Always remember that health is, to a point, relative. Just as we all look different, we're all born with a different set of hereditary and environmental circumstances. Some of us have a very healthy family background, with no cancer, heart disease, or other serious illnesses. Some of us live in healthier environments, with less pollution and violence and more family support. For those people, the chances of living a healthier, longer life are always better.

That's not to say that people with healthy histories living in healthy environments never die of cancer. It happens. It's one of those things we can't always control. However, we can always *increase* our chances of staying healthy by eating right, exercising regularly, managing stress, and so on.

Stress alone won't always make you sick. For example, if your grandfather developed a heart problem, it very well could be linked to his stressful life. However, chances are that he has physical problems that encourage heart disease, too. Maybe he doesn't eat or exercise the way he should. Or maybe his own dad had a heart problem—which he can't control. Risk factors add up, and a stress overload can add to those factors that lead to illness.

What's important to remember is that too much stress can precipitate a lot of different illnesses or disorders. Regardless of what your background might be, it's smart to keep your lifestyle under control. Give yourself the best chance for a long, healthy life (see "Nutrition" and "Exercise").

ENCYCLOPEDIA OF GOOD HEALTH

STRESS AND MENTAL HEALTH

Heavy stress over a long period of time can lead to a mental breakdown. A number of behavioral symptoms may indicate this health problem: shoplifting, addiction to drugs or alcohol, running away from home, eating binges, and other rebellious actions.

ENCYCLOPEDIA OF GOOD HEALTH
STRESS AND MENTAL HEALTH

Mood Disorders

We all have bad days—even bad weeks—now and then. Feeling happy or sad is a part of life. A negative mood is considered abnormal, or pathological, when it lasts too long, disrupts your life, or causes physical symptoms.

Depression is the most common disorder. You might say you're "depressed" when you have an argument with a friend, but depression as a mood disorder is much more serious. The causes are not completely understood. An inability to manage stress could cause a person to slip into depression. Doctors also say life history, psychological makeup, heredity, and even physical factors like hormone levels, allergies, and diseases could create depression.

The symptoms of depression are as follows:

- Feeling sad, hopeless, indifferent, numb, dull, tired, and/or empty for two weeks or more
- Inability to have a good time
- Sleeping too much or sleeping too little; not being able to fall asleep or waking up very early in the morning
- Loss of appetite and weight
- Crying or screaming
- Problems with concentration
- Bodily complaints: headaches, backaches, muscle cramps, nausea, vomiting, heartburn, shortness of breath, chest pains
- Loss of interest in school, activities, or work
- Loss of interest in appearance
- Avoiding friends and family
- Thoughts of death or suicide

How to deal with depression:

- Recognize the depression signals (above).
- Don't be afraid to cry.
- Get plenty of sleep and eat right.
- Talk out your problems with family and friends. Letting them know about the pressure you are feeling will make you feel better.
- Try to look at things more positively. Address the good points and benefits of what's going on in your life.
- Get in the habit of saying positive things about yourself.
- Try to get involved in something that really interests you: Join the Spanish club. Enroll in dance lessons. Get a job at the local animal shelter.
- Remember: Exercise is one of the best ways to control your mood and thus relieve depression.
- If depression doesn't go away, if physical problems persist, or if you can't eat or sleep properly, see a counselor or doctor.

Some of these symptoms could also be a sign of actual physical illness, so it is always wise to see a doctor.

(Left) Our need for close, loving friendships increases as we get older. Nurture your friendships; the people you meet now may be with you for the rest of your life.

ENCYCLOPEDIA OF GOOD HEALTH
STRESS AND MENTAL HEALTH

Teenage Suicide

In a cloud of carbon monoxide, a carload of New Jersey high-school students die in a closed garage. A California boy hangs himself in his own backyard. An Indiana girl slits her wrists and bleeds to death before she can be saved.

When we hear of such stories in the news, we are compelled to examine the causes of such tragic events. Unfortunately, you're living in a time when some people your age choose death as the answer to their problems. But is it? It is true, suicide will release you from stress, which seems overwhelming at times. If you were dead, you wouldn't have to face life's problems or worry about the future.

However, by escaping your own problems through suicide, you'll be leaving plenty of others behind. Think of your family and friends; they're going to have to deal with your death for years to come. Some will never get over it. Perhaps they'll even blame themselves. Some of your friends may even speak badly of you, thinking how selfish you were to leave them with guilt and bad memories.

However, the most important reason not to even consider taking such drastic action is that you owe it to yourself to work out your problems and prepare for an exciting future ahead of you. The good news is that things will get better. If you don't believe it, ask around. Life isn't always fair. We all have some bad experiences now and then, and day-to-day twists and turns can sometimes make life very hard. No one is denying that the kinds of problems teens encounter—pregnancy, loss of a boyfriend or girlfriend—are very troubling situations, but they can be solved without making life painful for you and those around you. You're a smart person; you can work it out. Remember: Most problems are temporary, but death is permanent. If those teens in the newspapers had truly made an effort to overcome their problems, they might be leading happy lives today.

Imprisonment is near the top of the stress scale.

ENCYCLOPEDIA OF GOOD HEALTH

STRESS AND MENTAL HEALTH

Suicide Signals

- Depression
- Threats or previous attempts to commit suicide
- Reading or writing about suicide
- Failure or poor performance at school
- Breaking off friendships
- Giving away possessions
- Complaints of sickness or illness
- Impulsive, hostile behavior
- Acting like a daredevil
- Change in eating or sleeping habits
- Increased drug, cigarette, or alcohol use
- Desire to punish oneself or others
- Low self-esteem
- Inability to concentrate
- Seeking out those who have attempted suicide

How to Help Someone Who Shows the Suicide Signals

Maybe all your friend needs is a shoulder to lean on, so listen to him or her. Chances are, you won't be able to solve your friend's problem, but it helps to talk about it. Whatever you do, don't say the problem is unimportant. To you, threatening suicide over a girlfriend or boyfriend may sound silly. To your friend, it's obviously a matter of life and death—for the time being.

Talk to your friend. Point out positive points to your friend: He or she is still healthy and has loving parents and friends who care about him or her very much. Emphasize that suicide is *not* the answer. Read "Teenage Suicide" (page 58) and tell him or her about the intense pain that family and friends suffer after someone they love commits suicide. Don't take the risk of daring your friend to commit suicide, however. Your reverse psychology technique may backfire. Don't make him or her feel worse by getting angry. Talk logically, but be sensitive.

Take action. If at any point you see warning signs that your friend may take action, don't hesitate to call in help. Try to get your friend to come with you to a counselor, doctor, or adult who can help. What if your friend won't come? Then don't try to handle this alone. Tell someone who will help your friend. Initially, your friend may be angry with you. But someday, when your friend is happy, alive, and well, he or she will thank you.

ENCYCLOPEDIA OF GOOD HEALTH

STRESS AND MENTAL HEALTH

How to Handle the Suicide of Someone You Know

As difficult as it may be, don't blame yourself for the death. In the best of circumstances, your perception and good intentions can fail. Most suicidal people drop all kinds of hints; in a way, they're subconsciously pleading for help. Others are very good at covering up their intentions, so that it's nearly impossible to save them.

No matter how you look at it, suicide was your friend's decision to take his life, and no one else's. He did it. You didn't. He had a weak spot and didn't think he could handle life. You can. It's sad, but true.

If you're having trouble dealing with someone's suicide, it's wise to talk to your friends and family about your feelings (a great way to handle any stressor). A visit to your counselor will probably do you good, too. At some point in our lives, most of us can use some professional help with emotional problems (see "Do I Need Professional Help?" page 93). The National Runaway Hotline will refer you to a hotline for professional help. Call 1-800-621-4000.

True or False?

People who attempt suicide usually don't talk about it.

False. In more than 80 percent of all cases, people who attempt suicide give out some definite signals (see "Suicide Signals," page 59).

True or False?

Once you get a suicidal person to feel better and stop talking about killing herself, the risk is over.

False. Most suicides occur within three months following the "improvement" period. You might think she's better, but she may be just finding the energy to try again.

The Danger of Group Behavior

One thing that psychologists have discovered in their research is that people do things as a group that individual members of that group would never do on their own. Groups tend to make people take more risks, behave without thinking, do things on a dare or do things to go along with the group and avoid embarrassment. The rock concert crowd that goes on a rampage is one example of group behavior. Other examples are the mass suicide of religious cult members or suicide pacts of some teenagers. These incidents show how individuals behaving in groups act differently than individuals.

The important thing to remember is that no one is totally immune to the influence of a group and you should be aware that what sounds attractive while you are part of a group may look differently if you take time to really think about it.

Anxiety disorders are another form of mood disorders that can be brought on by mismanaged stress. Anxiety is normal; it's the stress reaction we experience whenever we perceive danger. You feel anxious just before a test, whenever your dad is angry at you, or when you think about getting mugged.

Anxiety becomes abnormal when it interferes with daily functioning or emotional well-being. Serious anxiety disorders can make themselves known in two different ways:

1. Panic attacks. The symptoms of a panic attack are like the body's response to fight-or-flight situations. However, these mental and physical changes usually come on without warning and with tremendous impact. An overstressed person could be doing something as simple as folding her laundry when she experiences two or three of the following signs: shortness of breath, racing heart beat, chest pain or discomfort, smothering or choking sensation, dizziness, hot and cold flashes, excess perspiration, a feeling of unreality, trembling, nausea, vomiting, diarrhea, or fear of going crazy or dying.

2. Phobias. What are you afraid of: bats? heights? bugs? crowded rooms? Everyone has a few of those fears. When such fears dominate one's life, however, they become phobias. Often, phobias start suddenly as a result of a stressor. The victim is not only terrified of, for instance, snakes, but she's also afraid to go places where she thinks she'll find snakes, like the woods. She may even refuse to go on a trip to the zoo, fearing it might have snakes on display. Her phobia may even provoke panic attacks.

Plans of Action

Many times, these anxiety disorders can be handled without the help of a professional. The important thing to remember is that your fears are much greater than the actual threat of what causes them. The more you let your thoughts convince you to avoid something, the more afraid you will be of that event or object in the future. The best way to learn to handle them: Control. Here's what you can do:

Panic attacks:

(1) No matter how frightened you may feel, tell yourself that nothing will hurt you. (2) Try breathing and relaxation techniques to control your physical arousal (see pages 84 and 85). (3) Figure out what your stressor(s) may be, then take steps to remove or manage them.

Phobias:

(1) Use relaxation and breathing techniques when you're near the object that scares you. (2) Try to desensitize yourself: Look at pictures of whatever you fear. Once you can handle that, try facing up to it for a short time. Next, stand up to your phobia source for a longer time. (3) Think about your fears and go about proving to yourself that there's no reason for you to have them.

If both of these plans fail and your anxiety disorders are disrupting your life, seek professional help. We recommend a behavior therapist, usually a psychologist, with experience in anxiety disorders (see "Do I Need Professional Help?" page 93). The address for the national office of behavior therapists is:

American Association of Behavior Therapists
15 West 36th St.
New York, NY 10018

How to deal with tension at rush hour: Smile and relax as much as you can. If large crowds bother you try to adjust your schedule in order to avoid them. Allow yourself plenty of time to get where you're going.

THINGS ABOUT YOUR FAMILY THAT MAY CAUSE YOU STRESS

Studies show that people who live in happy families are better able to cope with stress. However, as a teen, you're probably starting to feel a little tension within your family. It seems like all you and your mom talk about is how messy your hair is and how you can't go to the football game because you got a "C" on your last algebra test. And forget your dad or your older brother—you can't talk to them at all. Ask your friends; they're probably going through the same thing. You're figuring out who you really are and that means breaking away from your family at times. Listed below are the areas in family relations where teens typically feel tension.

1. Manner and Morals: You may feel that your parents' standards are outdated and unnecessary.

2. Discipline At Home: If your parents discipline you the way they did when you were younger (send you to your room, for example), you may feel insulted or unfairly treated.

3. Personal Sensitivities: You may be overtly critical of your family life in general and in individual ways, which causes hostility within your family.

4. Family Rules: You probably have an increased desire for independence, so you clash with your parents over their rules.

5. Immature Attitudes: You may wish to be credited with more responsibility for your actions. However, you still sometimes neglect your homework or domestic chores, so it may seem that your parents want to have more control over you.

6. Sibling Rivalry: You may feel that the things your younger sister or brother does are stupid, and you may resent the privileges your older brother or sister gets (like going to that football game).

7. Family Responsibilities: When your whole family gets together it's just a bore, and if you didn't have to participate you wouldn't.

Remember that these are normal feelings during this time in your life. Don't let them cloud the fact that your family members are usually who you will turn to when you are really in trouble or in need.

Adapted from THE AMERICAN HEALTH FOUNDATION GUIDE TO LIFESPAN HEALTH.

ENCYCLOPEDIA OF GOOD HEALTH

STRESS AND MENTAL HEALTH

QUIZ: HOW VULNERABLE ARE YOU TO STRESS?

For some people, a little bit of stress goes a long way. Others can handle much bigger loads without blinking an eye. Why is this tolerance difference among individuals? It has to do with your health and heredity, your attitude, lifestyle, and your personality. Here's how to find out how sensitive you are to stress: Read each of the statements below and answer "Always," "Sometimes," or "Never" on your own piece of paper.

1. I get a good workout (jogging, sports, dancing) at least three times a week.
2. I am involved in clubs or groups (band, academic clubs, annual staff, etc.) in my school or community.
3. I talk to my parents or my brothers and sisters about my problems.
4. I avoid cigarettes and other tobacco products.
5. My doctor says my weight is about where it should be.
6. I have no problem giving or receiving affection.
7. I get enough sleep—at least eight hours a night.
8. I have at least one best friend who "understands" me.
9. I do something I enjoy (play ball, listen to music, see a movie, read a magazine) almost every day.
10. I drink fewer than two cola drinks or cups of tea or coffee each day.
11. There are tough times, but I basically like school.
12. I avoid drugs and alcohol.
13. Instead of holding all my problems inside, I talk to someone about them.
14. I feel like I am fairly popular at school; I have a group of friends who like me for what I am.
15. I have a good family life.
16. I am generally pleased with my appearance.
17. I am able to organize things: schoolwork, bedroom, time, etc.
18. I can put my problems in perspective and calm down when I need to.
19. My parents support me in what I do.
20. I find time to just be by myself.

SCORING

Score 5 points for each "Never," 3 points for each "Sometimes," and 1 point for each "Always." Total your points and subtract 20.

Over 75 points: You are extremely vulnerable to stress. Your answers will give you a clue as to what might increase your sensitivity. For example, if you said "Never" to "I am able to organize things," you know that organizational skills might reduce your stress. You'll find some help to this problem and others in the following section.

50–75 points: You are very vulnerable to stress. You, too, can learn something from your answers (see above). Of course, some problems you can't eliminate, but you usually can find a way to deal with them. The information on the next few pages will help you see the light.

30–49 points: You're somewhat sensitive to stress, as are most healthy people. But by taking a closer look at your answers, you might learn something about yourself. For example, if you answered "Sometimes" to "Instead of holding all my problems inside, I talk to someone about them," you've found a partial solution to stress. By sharing some of your problems, you'll have a lighter load to carry.

Under 30: Good job! You're in the best shape to handle a stressor. That's not to say you'll never have a stressful day in your life (that's impossible), but you don't invite stress into your life, either.

ENCYCLOPEDIA OF GOOD HEALTH
STRESS AND MENTAL HEALTH

If we know anything about health, we know that exercise is great for the body. It even helps you handle stress. Find out why on page 82.

STRESS AND YOUR BODY

Here are some of the ways stress can affect different parts of your body:

Hair
Some types of baldness are associated with severe stress.

Brain
Stress can induce many different problems, from anxiety to severe disorders such as schizophrenia.

Mouth
Problems such as ulcers can be a response to stress.

Respiratory System
Asthma attacks can be provoked in asthma sufferers.

Cardiovascular System
Heart attacks and other diseases of the heart and arteries are often linked to stress.

Digestive Tract
Indigestion can be a response to stress, as can more serious problems such as ulcers.

Bladder
Stress can cause an "irritable" bladder, especially in women.

Reproductive System
Changes include fertility problems in men and menstrual irregularities in women.

Muscles
Stress can intensify the tremor of Parkinson's Disease in sufferers and induce minor spasms and tics.

Skin
Stress can trigger problems such as eczema and psoriasis.

PART II:

What Can I Do To Control My Stress?

> **N**ow comes the fun part. After looking at stress and stressors in detail and how they fit into your life, you're going to use the next few pages to help you manage your stress. Basically, stressors can be handled in three different ways.

1. The Change-It Solution, in which you change, shut out, or escape the stressor.
2. The Mind-Over-Matter Solution, in which you change the way you feel or think about a stressor.
3. The Go-With-It Solution, in which you accept the stressor and try to physically release the stress it causes.

You can use a combination of all three solutions or just one or two to solve your stress problem. Different solutions work for different people. And different solutions work for different stressors. If your family is moving to a new town, you can't use solution #1; unless your family leaves you behind, you can't escape the move. However, you can use solution #2 by looking at the bright side: Mom's job in the new town will allow you to live better, you'll make new friends, and you'll be living close to the beach. Also, you could try talking about your fears with your family. At the same time, you can rely on #3 by starting an exercise program.

Part II is divided into sections that discuss these three solutions. Before you begin, take a moment to think about what stress situations you'd like to work on. Then try to apply what you read to your own life.

The Change-It Solution

How does this work? The Change-It Solution applies to foreseeable and avoidable stressors. Let's take four typical cases.

Roller coasters make you anxious. You know this amusement park thriller is a stressor because you experience all the fight-or-flight reactions. So to escape or avoid the stress, you escape or avoid the stressor. Change-It Solution: You don't go on roller coasters.

Being unprepared for Friday's history test is another stressor. You're going to change the nature of that stressor. Change-It Solution: You're going to *get* prepared for the test.

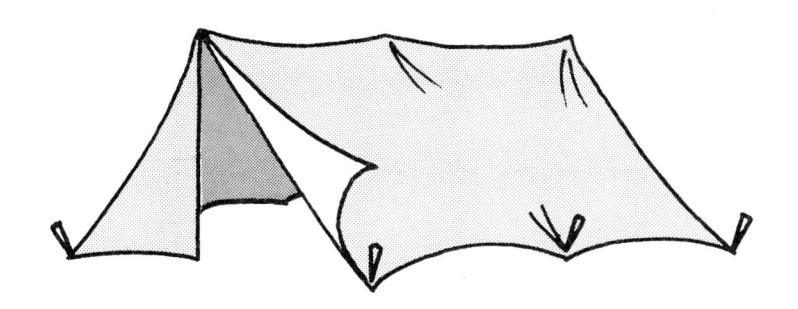

ENCYCLOPEDIA OF GOOD HEALTH
STRESS AND MENTAL HEALTH

You know drinking beer at the party can bring on stress. Why: You'll worry that your parents will find out or you'll get a bad reputation. So you put the Change-It Solution to work. You foresee that drinking beer will cause stress, so you choose to avoid your beer drinking buddies.

Some friends are planning to camp out on Saturday night, which sounds great, but you have to be at church bright and early to practice a solo. To be late or too tired would cause you stress. You can see this ahead of time. So how do you avoid stress? The Change-It Solution is to the stressor, which is not camping out on Saturday night. Sometimes, reducing stress means making sacrifices.

For many stressors, the Change-It technique is a good solution. For other stressors, however, this technique might not work. It will *not* apply if your stressor is foreseeable but not avoidable. You can anticipate such stressors, but you can't (or shouldn't) avoid them. You can foresee a history test, and in theory you could avoid it. In reality, however, you can't because you must attend school. Sometimes, a stressor is both unforeseeable and unavoidable. For example, you can't know that the bus will break down during your class trip. Or that Mom will get sick in 1990. In such situations, you must apply other solutions, which will be discussed later in this section.

These guys are probably drinking beer to help them relax. But taken in excess, alcohol damages the liver and impairs brain function.

71

General Stress-Avoidance Tactics
1. Plan ahead whenever you can. In all the situations described above, foresight would have helped you eliminate stress.
2. Organize your time and yourself. This enables you to deal with stressors in a neater, more orderly (thus, less stressful) way (see "Organizing Smarts," page 73).
3. Use good judgment. Some stressors you can avoid. Others you won't want to avoid (see "Being a Good Judge," page 74).
4. Space and pace your stressors. Stressors are less stressful when they don't come in bunches. For example, if you know you'll be training for the Junior Olympics throughout June, that might not be the best month to sign up for karate lessons and organize your class bake sale.
5. Avoid unnecessary chemical and physical stressors. You may decide auditioning for a local talent show is a stressor you don't want to avoid. But there's no need to increase your

stress level by passing up on sleep or by smoking cigarettes.
6. **Don't make impossible demands of yourself.** You may remember that Type A personalities tend to put themselves in overly stressful situations by taking on more than they can possibly handle. Get to know yourself and your limitations. Don't be afraid to say "no" (see "How To Say 'No,'" page 76).
7. **Recognize when you're getting in over your head.** Stress avoidance can sometimes be spontaneous. Even if you did sign up for too much work this year, it's not too late to reduce stress by cutting back, letting a few projects go. The smartest people recognize trouble when they see it—and act.

Organizing Smarts

All of the following situations are examples of how disorganization can cause stress:

- You forgot all about a term paper that's due in less than two days.
- The school bus will be here in ten minutes, but you can't find your homework in your messy room.
- You planned to meet your friends at the movies tonight, but you forgot that you agreed to baby-sit for a neighbor.

One of the best stress-avoidance skills is organization. Sometimes the best solutions to organizational problems are quite simple. For example, buying a small planning calendar will help you organize your time. In it you can write down all the important responsibilities and commitments you have for the future, including homework assignments and study times, dentist appointments, basketball games, and family get-togethers.

This tried-and-true organizational tactic will make life much less stressful. Get your own pocket-sized calendar and keep it in your locker or in your desk at home. When a teacher announces a test or essay, be sure to write it down. It's a good habit that will help you avoid stress for years to come. Note: Leave yourself more time than you think you need to get where you're going. If the basketball game starts at 8:00 don't expect to be home to study by 8:30. Feeling rushed or delayed can make you feel anxious, thus stressed. The calendar will also help you organize your homework. Lists can work wonders, too. Make a list of the books you have to take home over the weekend. List the supplies you have to buy for an English project. List the topics your teacher says will be included on the exam. And so on.

Another important aspect of your life is the organization of your bedroom. Not only will organizing your room allow you to find things when you need them, it might also help you work and relax. When clutter is all around, it's easy to get distracted from reading a textbook. Organizing your room can be as simple as placing things where they belong: clothes and shoes in the closet, tapes in the cassette case, books on the shelves, homework on your desk. It's easier to immediately hang up or toss clothes into a hamper than to (1) listen to Mom yell about the mess; (2) search through mountains of clothes to find your favorite sweatshirt; (3) pick up and separate a week's worth of clean *and* dirty clothes at the same time.

Being a Good Judge

Dilemma #1

What's more important: Getting your science project in on time or finishing your holiday gift shopping? Writing an important story for the newspaper or practicing for the tennis finals?

Being a good manager of stress means being a good judge. Your parents weigh many stressors each day, such as, is it more important for me to cook dinner tonight or meet my deadline tomorrow? Can I handle both? Because giving priorities to different projects becomes even more important as you get older, it's smart to learn this ability now.

Look at the questions at the beginning of this story. Which decisions would you make? Ask yourself these questions.

1. Can I manage to get my science project in on time *and* finish my shopping? Or would it be too stressful for me?
2. Is the science project more important or is shopping? What would benefit me most in the long run? In the short run? What would upset me most?
3. Will I have time to finish my science project tomorrow? Will the teacher penalize me for being late? Is there another time I can finish shopping?
4. How can I avoid having to make this decision next time—by starting my science project or shopping earlier in the holiday season? By working on my science project on weeknights and reserving the weekends for personal errands and recreation?

Unconsciously, you probably employ these judging and juggling strategies every day. By putting them to use as often as you can, you'll reduce stress. Ideally, you won't have to make these decisions too often; planning ahead and organizing your time can prevent you from having to forego tennis practice to write a newspaper story. For schedule conflicts you can't control, it helps to be a good judge.

Dilemma #2

You have shown star ability on the track. As the newest member on the team, you are the best hurdler. When you don't win a race, you always place. The coach and team members depend on you. Yet you're not so sure you enjoy being a star. You can't sleep at night because you're thinking about the races. You know you have to eat well in order to perform, but it's hard to eat when you're nervous. The stress is beginning to affect you negatively.

Many people would just accept this situation without questioning it, but being a good judge means weighing the importance of a stressor. Should you avoid it or not? Ask yourself these questions.

1. Is this stressor causing a comfortable amount of stress? Or is my body signaling a stress overload? (Review the signs on pages 42–44.)
2. Can I avoid other stressors (an art contest, baby-sitting) so this particular stressor has less impact?
3. If I avoided this stressor, would it cause other stressors (feeling left out, teammates' disappointment)?
4. Is this stressor important enough to me that I prefer to use other stress solutions (instead of avoiding the stressor, alleviate it by using relaxation techniques)?

Ultimately, it should be your decision. Put your health first. If a stressor makes you feel like you're on the brink of getting sick or losing control, you have to wonder if the stressor is worth risking your health. Some stressors, like your parents' divorce or death, you can't avoid. When you come across a stressor you can avoid, at least consider its importance.

Dilemma #3

Put one of your latest stressors in this spot. Ask yourself some judgment questions. Then decide whether this stressor should be avoided or dealt with in other ways. If you can't use the Change-It Solution on your stressor, then maybe the Mind-Over-Matter Solution (page 79) or the Go-With-It Solution (page 82) will work.

Although being a star athlete has its advantages, this position can also result in a lot of tension. Junior high jocks, then, should make allowances for the added pressure. Look for ways to relax.

How to Say "No"

Studies show that we are more vulnerable to stress when we feel out of control—as if we can't change the situation we're in or when we can't predict what is going to happen to us. Sometimes we can't. But many times we can. Even if you can't change a situation—like acne or a handicap—you can definitely change the way you feel about it, the way you handle it. Likewise, rather than not knowing when you will have to deal with some consequences for past activities, confront the situation head-on so you can predict what and when something will occur. If there's anything you should take with you when you close this book, it's the knowledge that *you are in control*. You have the power to make your life go the way you want it to. True, you don't have the power to stay thirteen forever, but you do have the power to make the years ahead rewarding ones.

One way to stay in control is to say "no" to demands that other people make of you or even to say "no" to yourself when you feel as if you're not in control of a situation. No, I will not have sex with you. No, you cannot copy my homework. No, I won't worry about how my hair looks. No, I won't let others' criticism of me upset me. Is it easy or difficult for you to say "no?" Here are some hints for saying "no" to yourself or to others.

1. Look at the stressful situations in your life. How do you ordinarily handle them? Do you try to avoid conflict (say, smoking cigarettes because you don't feel like telling your friends why you'd rather not)? Do you try to please others? Do you refuse to recognize that you have your stress limits?
2. Think about stressful situations in your life and determine which ones could be eliminated or reduced by your saying "no." Perhaps it's a friend who expects you to dislike certain people or a club that you don't like being a member of.
3. *Imagine* yourself handling the problem; telling your friend you will not be mean to someone she disapproves of or writing a letter of resignation to the club president. Picture how your friend or the club president would react to you. Using imagery is a great way to predict consequences and make them less scary.

4. Practice this in front of a mirror—even if you're simply telling yourself, "No, I will not get upset over this bad grade." It helps you to see how strong you can be.
5. Practice saying "no" to a family member or friend.
6. If you're saying "no" to another person and not to yourself now try doing the real thing. Try to actually use the word "no." Say, "No, Kelly, I won't ignore Pat because you don't like her." This is more convincing than, "Well, Kelly, I guess I can see why you don't like Pat, but we don't have to be mean about this, do we?"
7. Be as brief as possible. Long excuses and apologies encourage others to try to change your mind. Politely yet directly state what you plan to do and why you plan to do it. Example: "Kevin, I'm dropping out of the club. I've lost interest in collecting bottle caps."
8. If someone does try to change your mind, repeat your "no" answer. This works even when you try to change *your own* mind about a decision you've made. Tell yourself, "No, I will not worry about this situation, and that's that." Silence helps, too. If someone insists on trying to convince you to do something against your will and you have already stated your case, simply let the person talk. At the same time, repeat to yourself over and over, "No, thank you."

Facing Up to What You Really Can't Change

Some things are forced on us: accidents, illness, and so on. Strength comes from accepting these incidents and relying on stress solutions to deal with them. Here's a nice philosophy to help you handle these situations:

Serenity Prayer

God grant me the serenity
To accept the things I cannot change,
The courage to change the things I can,
And the wisdom to know the difference.

Theologian Reinhold Niebuhr

ENCYCLOPEDIA OF GOOD HEALTH

STRESS AND MENTAL HEALTH

In junior high, having a date for the dance can seem like the most important thing in the world. But it doesn't have to be an extremely stressful situation. See page 79.

The Mind-Over-Matter Solution

The Change-It Solution eliminates a stressor. But when you can't avoid a stressor or when you choose to accept it, the Mind-Over-Matter Solution helps you feel better about your situation. Here are two cases in which this solution is appropriate:

Not having a date for the dance is causing you stress. You did all you could to eliminate the stressor (Change-It Solution) by asking someone to go with you, but he or she already had plans. How can you best manage this stressor? Mind-Over-Matter Solution: Make yourself feel better by looking at this situation logically. The worst that can happen is that you'll go to the dance alone. No doubt there are plenty of other people who are going alone—why not buddy up with them? This way you'll be able to dance with more than one person. (Note: Experience tells us you may have a problem with this one. In junior high, having a date for the dance can seem like the most important thing in the world. We understand, but what good will feeling depressed do? Do your best to shake this off with the Mind-Over-Matter Solution. If you try hard enough, you just may end up having a great time!)

Playing the lead in the school play is a big responsibility. You've considered using the Change-It Solution and avoiding it, but you decided the play is important to you and worth the stress. However, you still feel anxious. Mind-Over-Matter Solution: You're going to make yourself feel better about the play. Right now you're very worried about the situation and think you might forget your lines. To stop your worrying, simply practice your lines over and over. At the same time, put the situation in perspective and try to see it for what it is. The school play isn't a Broadway production. Take pride in your performance, and learn from your mistakes so that you can do better next time. Realize what a compliment it was to be chosen for this role. By practicing and talking yourself into a positive frame of mind, you've effectively used the Mind-Over-Matter Solution to turn stress into a positive experience.

As you can see, positive thinking is everything when it comes to managing stress. The success of the Mind-Over-Matter Solution depends on your attitude. To help your positive thinking, look for positive actions. For example, in the first situation, you linked up with other singles at the dance. This made you feel better about going to the dance alone—it put a positive light on the situation. To deal with the second problem, you practiced your theater lines over and over. This gave you confidence and less cause for worry.

Using these examples, you can see how the Mind-Over-Matter Solution can make a difficult situation into an enjoyable experience.

A Dose of Humor

When's the last time you had a good, old-fashioned, belly laugh? It felt good, didn't it? Believe it or not, doctors recommend laughter as a stress manager. Laughter has a relaxing effect on the body—perhaps even a healing one. A magazine editor named Norman Cousins claims he overcame a crippling disease with the help of laughter. A group in California meets on a regular basis to tell jokes, see funny movies, and hopefully laugh away cancer. It isn't clear if humor actually hinders disease, but it certainly doesn't hurt. At least, we know that it makes us feel better on a daily basis.

Granted, there will be days when laughter will not necessarily solve all your problems, yet you will no doubt feel better by looking for the humorous side of things.

ENCYCLOPEDIA OF GOOD HEALTH

STRESS AND MENTAL HEALTH

It's All in Your Head

Grace hears a noise and her heart skips a beat. Lying very still in her bed, her eyes widen in fear, she listens to see if she had only imagined the sound. Another carpet-quieted step and a creak of the stairs tells her she isn't mistaken. Struggling to stifle her heavy breathing and an instinct to scream, Grace looks to the window. Should she jump to safety? Or should she hide under the bed and hope to go unnoticed?

Sheila hears a noise and sits up. She listens intently and hears another carpet-quieted step and a creak of the stairs. Calmly considering the possibilities, she gets out of bed to see who is there, knowing it is likely to be one of her parents going to bed or her brother trying to keep it a secret that he got in late.

What's different about these two stories? Grace's perception of the noise. In the first paragraph, Grace experiences the fight-or-flight reaction because she hears an unfamiliar noise. In the second paragraph, Sheila remains cool: The situation isn't stressful for her. Why? Because she uses reason and knows that the sound is probably only a family member going to bed.

The point: Stress is aroused in situations we perceive to be dangerous. If you really are in danger, then by all means, respond. In most situations, however, you aren't in real danger; you only think you are. This is where the Mind-Over-Matter Solution will help you. Take control of your thoughts and you'll take control of your stress.

The Go-With-It Solution

When the body experiences the fight-or-flight reaction, it produces energy. You'll remember that in prehistoric times this excess energy was necessary for survival. Today, the stress reaction can help us play a great basketball game or run from a thief, but stress energy doesn't get significantly used up when we're going about our everyday activities. At the same time, we can't avoid every stressful situation in order to avoid the physical stress reaction.

So what do we do? We find ways to reduce our stress levels. How you might do that is up to you. Here are two typical cases that show how to use the Go-With-It Solution to alleviate stress:

You are about to take a difficult math test. You have already prepared for the situation through using the Change-It Solution and studying and through using the Mind-Over-Matter Solution and thinking positive thoughts. However, you still have excess energy that you need to channel productively. Go-With-It Solution: Do breathing and relaxation exercises before class.

You are feeling tense because you just moved into a new neighborhood. The Change-It Solution has already helped you make new friends by motivating you to introduce yourself to other students at school. The Mind-Over-Matter Solution has also given you a brighter mental outlook. But you still feel on edge. Go-With-It Solution: Join the school tennis team, which helps release pent-up energy through exercise and allows you to meet new people.

Exercise

We already know that physical activity strengthens our heart, makes us stronger and more toned, and helps fight diseases (see "Exercise"). Now we can look to exercise as a top-notch cure for stress. Some of its benefits:

- Exercise "spends" the stress energy our body makes but doesn't always get a chance to use.
- Exercise physically relaxes the muscles that tense with stress.
- Exercise has an effect on the mind. Physically, exercise works on a part of the brain that determines your mood. Mentally, you'll have a chance to forget about your problems while you concentrate on the activity.
- Exercise puts you in better physical condition, and therefore prepares you to resist stress and strain.
- Exercise can be participatory, which means you interact with other people. This in itself is a great stress-reducer.

For these and a host of other healthy reasons, one of the smartest things you can do now is begin a regular exercise program—three times a week minimum! Find your ideal activity in "Exercise," and get started.

ENCYCLOPEDIA OF GOOD HEALTH
STRESS AND MENTAL HEALTH

A number of studies have shown that physical activity ''spends'' stress energy and helps the body return to a normal state after a tense situation (see ''Exercise''). People with emotional disorders often improve when involved in regular running, bicycling, or swimming programs. Furthermore, a Michigan research team recently reported that exercisers seem to make friends more easily and have better personal relationships. The explanations for these findings are complicated, but the message is clear: Exercise is great for your mind.

ENCYCLOPEDIA OF GOOD HEALTH

STRESS AND MENTAL HEALTH

Breathing and Stretching

We can't emphasize exercise enough, but such vigorous activities as swimming or running aren't the only answers. When a strenuous workout isn't practical or desirable, you can turn to breathing and stretching techniques. Some can be done just about anywhere. Simply following these easy steps:

1. Breathe in and concentrate on your face, neck, shoulders, and arms for tension. Become fully aware of how your face, neck, shoulders, and arms feel, concentrating on any tightness. Breathe out slowly, feeling the tension in these areas slip away. Release the muscles until they're completely slack. Do this again with your chest, lungs, and stomach. Then your hips, legs, and feet. You have to fully concentrate to get this to work.

2. Lie on your back on the floor. Close your eyes and picture yourself in the most stressful situation you can think of. Keep this idea in your mind and clench your teeth and fists. Scrunch your shoulders and point your toes as much as you can. Push yourself to an even tenser state. Now take a long, slow, deep breath, at the same time unclench your fists, let your toes go limp, wriggle and lower your shoulders. Switch the picture in your mind to a comforting one. It could be sunbathing on a quiet beach. Or sleeping in a soft bed. Keep breathing deeply and keep thinking this nice fantasy.

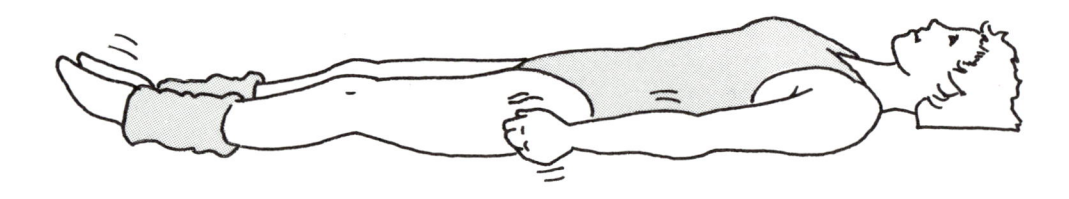

You can try stretching exercises at home or join a health club. Many clubs have stretch classes in addition to aerobics.

84

3. (a) Roll your head slowly clockwise then counterclockwise, three times each way. (b) Slowly drop your head forward and then to each side as far as possible. Repeat this ten times. (c) Keeping your head level, turn it side to side ten times slowly, then ten times quickly. (d) Shrug both shoulders together. Then take turns shrugging each shoulder. Raise them high, then let them drop heavily. (e) Sit in a firm, upright chair. Slowly raise your arms behind the back of the chair, firmly clasping your hands. Squeeze your shoulder blades together. Gradually lean backward, arching your upper back over the chair.

4. Breathe in through your nose counting slowly and steadily to four. Concentrate on pressing down your abdominal muscles so your stomach protrudes as you inhale and fill your lungs. Hold your breath for a count of four. As you do, be aware of your ribs; they should feel like a balloon blowing up at the front and back of your body. Now begin to breathe out, counting slowly and steadily to four. Do this until you empty your lungs completely. If you feel dizzy or faint, stop immediately. Try again in a minute, if dizziness persists see your physician. If you feel fine, try this again.

5. (a) Stretch both arms up toward the ceiling with hands and fingers outstretched. Keep stretching as far as you can. Then droop, relax, and release. Repeat. (b) Pretend you have a pencil on the tip of your chin. With that imaginary pencil, write your name in the air. Use wide, sweeping motions to stretch your neck and shoulder muscles. (c) Pretending you have a pencil on your right elbow, write a friend's name in the sky. Repeat with your left elbow. (d) Write the name again with your left hip, then your right hip.

A great daydream—winning an Olympic medal!

Daydreaming

Want to take a break from the action? Fantasize!

The power of your daydreams is amazing. By emptying your mind and directing your thoughts away from whatever is bothering you, you can solve your problems, relieve boredom, defuse anger, ward off tension, and reach a very comfortable level of relaxation. Use daydreams or fantasies to fill up time (waiting in lines, sitting in study hall), release yourself from a stressful situation (occupying yourself while waiting your turn in the trumpet tryouts) or just to amuse yourself. How-to's:

- Think of happy events, joyful feelings, or peaceful scenes to relax the muscles in your head. Examples: a holiday dinner with your family, or swimming in the ocean.
- To pull yourself out of a bad mood, dwell on a fantasy that encourages self-esteem. Examples: winning an Olympic medal or being noticed by a Hollywood talent scout.
- Diminish anger and stress by conjuring up satisfying fantasies. Example: Your math teacher humiliated you by making you work out a problem on the blackboard until you got it right—in front of the whole class. You imagine not only solving the problem, but also embarrassing the teacher by showing him how he made mistakes when he did it.
- Use the power of your mind to improve your performance in something. If you want to be the best singer in the school, dream of yourself that way.

ENCYCLOPEDIA OF GOOD HEALTH
STRESS AND MENTAL HEALTH

Our happiness and emotional security depend on the way we relate to others. Experts say the first step to getting along with others is to accept and like yourself.

Relax

When you're in the middle of a stressful situation, you can use any of the techniques in "Breathing and Stretching" or "Daydreaming" (see pages 84 and 87) to help you relax. If you need something less demanding but more calming, try this exercise:

Sit down calmly. Put your hands firmly on a table or desk and say "Stop!" Don't cross your knees; just keep your body relaxed and breathe slowly and rhythmically. Focus your gaze on an object: perhaps your shoe or a pencil. Study it. Look at every little detail: how it's shaped, how it smells. Imagine what it feels like. Keep concentrating on it. Describe it to yourself and what it means to you. (This is my shoe. It's black, soft, smells like leather, etc.) Do this for five minutes and you should feel calm afterwards.

People Support

Another effective way to deal with stress is by reaching out to others. Studies show people who live alone tend to have higher stress levels. As human beings, we thrive on interpersonal ties. We need people to give us emotional support, feedback, and assistance. What's more, we need to *give*, to feel needed. Doctors believe that people who lack this social interaction are more vulnerable to diseases of the body and mind (see "Lack-of-People Pressure," page 33).

How can you make people support work? First, by sharing your problems with others. Bottling up your emotions increases stress, so it's important to talk about them whenever possible. Even when others can't solve your problem, it helps to "get if off your chest."

Work hard to keep your relationships with family and friends healthy. When you're part of a loving "team," you feel important. Relationships just don't happen, though. You have to give them your love and attention, or else they don't survive. If you've ever been in a one-sided relationship—you're always giving but she's always taking—you know what it's like to be on the other end. When a friend or family member is in a stressful situation, you have to be able to offer assistance and advice, too. This strengthens a relationship and ensures that she'll help you when you're having problems.

Another way to relieve stress is to forget about yourself and do something nice for someone else. Remember the last time you gave a gift to someone or did a favor for no special reason? It should have made you feel great about yourself. Doing for others is good therapy.

Look to your home, school, church, community, and any other group for people support. If your family is lacking in closeness, then try to transform your friends into "relatives." You'll not only have an outlet to relieve stress, you'll prevent some of it.

QUIZ: PEOPLE SUPPORT

1. Do you belong to any school clubs?
   (Give yourself 2 points for every club you belong to. Add 1 additional point if you are an officer or highly active in the club, meaning you attend every meeting and participate in the club functions.)
2. Do you belong to a religious group?
   (Give yourself 2 points if the answer is "yes." Add 1 additional point if you attend and participate at least once a week.)
3. Do you belong to any community groups (Boy Scouts, charities, etc.)?
   (Give yourself 2 points for every group you belong to. Add 1 additional point if you are an officer or highly active in the group.)
4. Do you belong to any other groups?
   (Same scoring as above.)
5. How many close friends—people you can trust and talk to—do you have?
   (If you have 3, give yourself 3 points. 10 friends? Give yourself 10 points. And so on.)
6. How many relatives do you feel close to?
   (Same scoring as above.)
7. How many of these friends or relatives do you see at least once a month?
   (Same scoring as above.)
8. How often do you exchange letters and/or talk on the telephone with close friends or relatives?
   (Once a week or more, 4 points; a few times a month, 3 points; once a month, 2 points; less, 1 point.)

SCORING

45 or more points: High support. You have a well-developed network of people to help you handle stress.

24–44 points: Moderate support. You seem to have enough people behind you, but it wouldn't hurt to strengthen your people-support system.

Below 25 points: Low support. Reach out! If you're having trouble with your support network, you may need professional help (see "Do I Need Professional Help?" page 93).

ENCYCLOPEDIA OF GOOD HEALTH
STRESS AND MENTAL HEALTH

WHAT IS LACK-OF-PEOPLE PRESSURE?

The photograph above shows a typical situation in which several people shape and influence the decisions of others. Everyday, in situations as common as choosing a videotape or deciding what to eat in a restaurant, you use the attitudes of the people you know and respect to help you establish your own attitude. However, at times, worrying about what other people think will weigh on you to the point that you can't make a clear decision. If this is the case, spend some time alone and think it through by yourself.

There's a flip side to the realities and problems of people pressure, though—lack-of-people pressure. As discussed on page 33, being away from the influence of other people for a very long time has been shown in scientific studies to be even more stressful than being with too many people. But lack-of-people pressure doesn't just occur when someone is alone on a desert island; it can happen to anyone, in the midst of an otherwise normal day-to-day life. See the list below for some typical examples of lack-of-people pressure situations.

1. Feelings like you don't have any friends
2. Moving to a strange new city or a new school
3. Getting grounded for a month or more—no exceptions
4. Not talking to anyone for a while
5. Going to jail
6. Feeling like no one understands you
7. Not having a family
8. Getting lost for a long time
9. Getting kicked out of school
10. Being away from your family for a long time

ENCYCLOPEDIA OF GOOD HEALTH
STRESS AND MENTAL HEALTH

When you have a problem, it's sometimes better to talk to someone other than family members or friends. The closer you are to someone, the harder it may be for him or her to help. See page 93 for some ideas on whom to turn to for advice.

Do I Need Professional Help?

There may come a time in your life when your stressors are too much for you to handle and you need some outside help. It's nothing to be ashamed or scared of; all of us feel overstressed every once in a while. If you're smart enough to realize that you can't get through a stressful period alone, you should be proud—not everybody recognizes his or her limitations, and ignoring a need for help can be disastrous. After all, if you were injured or ill, you would do something about it, right? Psychological problems sometimes need the same professional attention as physical ones.

How can you tell when you might need professional help? Ask yourself these questions:

1. Have you tried unsuccessfully to manage the problem yourself?
2. Have you talked with friends and family and allowed them to advise other strategies? Did you try them and find them to be unsuccessful as well?
3. Are you feeling overwhelmed, as if your choices are becoming narrower?
4. Have you begun to suffer physically? (See the symptoms, page 42-44.)

Positive answers to these questions indicate that you might benefit from professional help. Here's what to do: First, talk to your parents. They should have some leads about whom you should see. If they fail to see the seriousness of your situation, then turn to your school counselor, a clergyman, or family doctor. Maybe a few good talks with one of these experts will set you on your way to feeling better. Or maybe one will suggest that you see a therapist.

It is likely that you'll find some guidance from one of these people. If you want to explore therapy on your own, use the behavior therapy referral number on page 63, call the psychology department of a nearby university or community hospital, or your county's Mental Health Association for references. Some doctors offer low rates through community programs.

If all else fails, or if you ever feel you need immediate help, call a crisis center hotline. These people are trained to talk out your problems and will be glad to hear from you. Check your phone book or call the operator for the number.

With the ever-growing problem of teen depression and suicide has come greater public awareness. Consequently, you probably won't have to look far to find someone eager to work with you. Take advantage of that helping hand. A lot of people care about you.

ENCYCLOPEDIA OF GOOD HEALTH

STRESS AND MENTAL HEALTH

Mismanaging Stress

We've talked extensively about good ways to handle stress. Now, here are ways to mismanage stress that you should avoid. They'll only harm your health and are no way to cope with stress:

- Using drugs, alcohol, or tobacco to help you relieve tension
- Blaming others for your stress
- Trying to avoid hassles by avoiding people
- Overworking
- Taking yourself too seriously
- Missing out on rest and good nutrition
- Holding your problems inside
- Ignoring stress signals
- Failing to seek help when you need it
- Committing suicide

Write Your Own Relaxation Plan

Relaxation means different activities to everyone. It's not important how you relax, just be sure to do it. All work and no play will make you dull *and* stressed-out! Get in the habit of fitting recreation into your schedule every day. Sometimes it's better for you to compromise on your homework standards and enjoy life than to be a perfectionist and ruin your health. Some relaxing ideas:

- Listen to music
- Play with children or animals
- Rest in a bath, steamroom, or sauna
- Read books or magazines
- Spend time in a park or outdoors enjoying nature
- Cook
- Enjoy a craft or hobby
- Take naps or sunbathe
- Play a musical instrument
- Watch television
- Work in the yard or garden
- Write in a journal or notebook
- Attend theater, concerts, or shows
- Ride a bike
- See a sports event
- Do yoga

Can You Do It?

Step by step, page by page, we've gone through a problem-solving process that should help you work through your daily stressors. If it helps, take a sheet of paper and apply this procedure to something that is causing you stress right now.

1. Stop and listen to your body talk. How do you know you're feeling stressed? Do you feel any of the fight-or-flight physical reactions (see page 15)? Do you feel psychological, physical, or behavioral symptoms (pages 48–50)? Write them down.
   Possible answers: I feel anxious. A little worried. Sometimes my head hurts.
2. Define the stressor. What is stressing you?
   Possible answers: I'm insecure about my looks because I have acne.
3. Try the Change-It Solution. What can you do to change, escape, or avoid the situation?
   Possible answers: The Change-It Solution—I could try to change my looks by washing my face every morning and night with soap and water, avoid touching my face with my hands (it spreads dirt), apply medicated skin-care creams, and eat the right foods.
4. Try the Mind-Over-Matter Solution. What can you do to change the way you feel about this situation?
   Possible answers: The Mind-Over-Matter Solution—I could tell myself that acne isn't such a terrible problem. After all, most kids my age have complexion problems. I will grow out of it. In the meantime, I'll concentrate on staying in shape, taking the best care that I can of my complexion, taking good care of my hair and teeth, and developing a great personality and sense of humor.
5. Try the Go-With-It Solution. How can you relieve your stress?
   Possible answers: The Go-With-It Solution—After school I'll take time to relax before I start homework. Also, I'll be sure to take a jog around the block three times a week.

You're so busy with school and all the things that junior-high students do, you might forget that you need to relax, too. Take a break every now and then. You're in charge of your own health; parents aren't able to read your mind and know when you're overworked.

You've just worked out a plan to combat your stress. In this case, we were able to use all three solutions to work out a solution to stressor-related worrying. However, you may have found that all three solutions didn't help; maybe one or two did. In any case, explore all your avenues. That is, if you do have three good solutions, try all three of them. If you have only one, use it to its fullest. If you find that one Go-With-It Solution doesn't work, devise another plan. If a Change-It Solution doesn't change the situation, maybe another idea is in order.

Here are a few other daily problems. We've tried to apply a problem-solving technique to all of them, which may or may not work. You'll see that in some situations, it's important to weigh alternatives before deciding which solution is best (review "Being a Good Judge," page 74):

Stress symptom: You can't sleep at night, so you're always tired in the daytime.

Stressor: Your dog barks all night and keeps you awake.

1. Change-It: Disciplining the dog to make him stop barking is one possible solution here. Other Change-It Solutions are to have the dog taken away or to move away from the dog. However, because the dog is your pet, you cannot act on these—nor would you want to. Be a good judge. It doesn't hurt to write down all kinds of solutions, but you'll have to weigh the consequences of some possibilities. You'll probably decide to explore other options.

2. Mind-Over-Matter: Instead of feeling uptight, convince yourself that a dog's bark is a nice sound; it comes with living in the country. Also, you can be sure that you're safe with the dog patrolling the grounds.

3. Go-With-It: Do breathing, stretching, and relaxation exercises to calm down. Being fully relaxed will make you less sensitive to loud noises so you can drift off to sleep.

Stress symptom: You've been depressed for some time.

Stressor: Your grandfather's death.

1. Change-It: In this case, you can't bring back the person you love. You could ignore the fact that he died, but that's not a healthy solution. In order to go on, we have to accept death as a normal part of life.

2. Mind-Over-Matter: Reason with yourself. Think, "It was very sad that Grandpa died, but it's not the end of the world. In time, I know I won't feel so sad. For now I should remember how happy he was with Grandma. We shared good times together; I was a good grandson to him. We all have to die someday, and Grandpa understood that." Talk to your parents, sister, brother, and friends about how much you miss your grandfather, and your good memories of him.

3. Go-With-It: Exercise daily to release pent-up stress energy.

Stress symptom: You feel anxious and insecure. You worry a lot—so much that your parents frequently ask if you're okay.

Stressor: You want to be popular. You're bothered by the fact that you're not included in a certain group at school.

1. Change-It Solution: Find out what this crowd likes to do, then do it. For example, if they're athletic, you might join a team. Perhaps you'll have to change your style in clothes, make straight A's, or smoke cigarettes. (Be a good judge!)
2. Mind-Over-Matter: Reason with yourself. Ask "Why do I want to be a part of this group? Are their principles sound?" (Hint: If cigarettes or clothes or money are what binds them together, maybe they're not worth your time.) Think through the problem and maybe you'll decide that if getting "in" with these people is so difficult, they're not the best crowd for you.
3. Go-With-It: Spend more time with your present friends and get to know them better. Maybe they're more fun for you to be with, anyway. Remember: Relationships are an important way to curb stress.

Stress symptom: You're irritable—very.

Stressor: Your mother gets mad at you a lot.

1. Change-It Solution: Move out of the house. (Be a good judge.) Stop doing things that anger your mother. Stay away from her whenever she's mad. Ask her to try to control herself.
2. Mind-Over-Matter: Tell yourself that she's only human; she isn't necessarily annoyed with you. When other things are wrong in people's lives, they sometimes take them out on those who are close to them. Maybe you could talk to Mom and find out what's going on, which would help you to change the way you feel about this situation.
3. Go-With-It: Get out of the house and go for a walk. Spend some "quiet time" playing with your kid brother.

ENCYCLOPEDIA OF GOOD HEALTH

STRESS AND MENTAL HEALTH

ARE YOU DEPRESSED?

Sometimes you or a friend are feeling down, not on top of things. Maybe you're disappointed that you're not going to the dance on Friday night or you're having a hard time in biology. Everybody has these low times; they pass eventually, and you'll feel good again. However, sometimes people are very depressed, and then their condition has very real physical and emotional signs. The chart below points out some of these signs and compares them to normal reactions. Use it to help recognize when you or someone you care about is depressed and needs help.

Stimulus, Goal, or Physical Function	Normal Response	Depressed Response
Attitude toward a loved one or friend	Fondness or pleasure	Indifference or revulsion
Things you like to do	Enjoyment	Lack of enthusiasm
Humorous events	Pleasure	Dullness
Getting what you want	Pleasure	Withdrawal
Survival	Self-preservation	Apathy or suicide
Hopes for the future	Optimistic	Pessimistic
Response to life's events	Realistic	Defeatist
Appetite	Hungry at normal times	Loss of appetite
Sleep	Satisfying	Hard to sleep
Energy level	Sufficient or high	Low or tired

ENCYCLOPEDIA OF GOOD HEALTH

STRESS AND MENTAL HEALTH

Schoolwork is bound to make you anxious. But if you try the Mind-Over-Matter Solution (page 79), you might find that studying helps you cope with stress.

Stressor Directory

Throughout these pages, we've mentioned a multitude of the daily hassles you may be dealing with. If you're interested in what we said about them, this directory should help.

Accidents	36
Boy/girlfriends	25, 36, 98
Dates	36, 79
Death	30, 36, 97
Divorce	30, 36, 44
Environment	30, 36
Exhaustion	36, 97
Family	26, 32, 36
Friends	22, 32, 36
Grades	36
Injuries and illnesses	30, 36, 53, 54, 57
Insecurity	33, 36
Moving	36, 82
Music and drama performance	79
New family member	26, 30, 36
New school	16, 36
Noise	30
Parents	16, 36
School elections	16
Schoolwork	22, 36, 74
Sex	36
Sports performance	20, 36, 75
Substance abuse	28, 35, 36, 47
Teachers	36
Violence	19, 70, 82
Weight problem	28

Staying in Control

If you have read all of these pages, you're one well-informed person. Armed with this knowledge, you should be able to handle most of today's stressors. But if you should ever feel overwhelmed and very unhappy, don't be afraid to admit it. As we've pointed out before, most of us need help in dealing with life's crises. Get help when you need it. After all, we live in a complicated world.

Also, remember this: You have a great deal of control over your life, and you should never hesitate to use it. The stress management tips on these pages will help you exercise that control to your best benefit. You'll only be a junior-high-school students for a few short years; do all you can to make them happy ones.

GLOSSARY

Adrenal gland A hormone-making part of the body found above the kidneys and beneath the lungs. It produces adrenalin.

Ailment A bodily disorder or disease.

Apathy A lack of interest, concern, emotion, or feeling.

Ambitious Having a strong desire to reach a particular goal.

Anxiety An intense, uneasy feeling about something.

Asthma A condition of the muscles in the walls of the lungs that makes it difficult to breathe.

Blood The fluid that circulates in the heart and vessels of a vertebrate animal, carrying food and oxygen to, and waste from, all parts of the body.

Caffeine A mild stimulant found in tea, coffee, cocoa, chocolate, and cola drinks. See "Nutrition" and "Substance Abuse."

Cancer A group of diseases characterized by the uncontrolled and irregular growth of abnormal cells. See "Nutrition" and "Exercise."

Cardiovascular Relating to the heart and blood vessels.

Chronic Something, often an illness or bodily disorder, that lasts for a long period of time and/or keeps coming back.

Circulatory system The heart, blood, and blood vessels, which carry nutrients to, and waste from, all parts of the body.

Colitis Inflammation or irritation of the colon. The colon is the part of the large intestine that extends to the rectum. Just before waste passes out of the body, it passes through the colon.

Composure A state of being calm or "pulled together."

Constipation When dry, hard body waste is passed out of the body infrequently or abnormally, a person is constipated. Often, this condition is caused by a low-fiber diet or not drinking enough liquid. See "Nutrition."

Contemporary Marked by characteristics of the present time.

Crisis An emotional event or big change that must be handled immediately. A person in a crisis may want to get help from someone trustworthy and knowledgeable.

Cult A group of persons dedicated to the same beliefs and, sometimes, to a leader. Usually, the group is small and extremely loyal to its purpose.

Depressant A drug that causes the activity of the nervous system (the brain and spinal cord) to slow down. Alcohol is an example of a depressant. See "Substance Abuse."

Diabetes A disease in which the body cannot use sugar from food properly.

GLOSSARY

Digestion The process of breaking food down into simple substances so it can be absorbed into the bloodstream and carried to all parts of the body. See "Nutrition."

Dilate To become enlarged.

Drug Any chemical other than food that is purposely taken into the body to affect its normal processes. See "Substance Abuse."

Fatigue A feeling of extreme tiredness and weariness that usually comes from work or exertion.

Goose bumps A temporary rough and bumpy condition of the skin, usually caused by fear or cold.

Heredity The passing on of different traits from parents to offspring through the genes. Genes are tiny, complicated "patterns" that determine what a person is. For example, if you have your father's green eyes, they were probably passed on via his genes. Likewise, we can inherit certain health problems such as cancer and heart disease through the genes.

High blood pressure, or hypertension Blood pressure is the pressure of blood against the walls of the arteries. When a person exercises or becomes excited, this pressure goes up. But an abnormal condition called high blood pressure occurs when pressure stays high all the time. See "Nutrition" and "Exercise."

Hormones Body chemicals produced by several glands. Hormones move through the bloodstream and are the force behind most of the body's systems.

Hostility When a person is hostile or shows hostility, he acts as if others around him are enemies.

Hyperventilation If you breathe in too much oxygen too fast, you could hyperventilate. You may then experience dizziness or faintness.

Hypothalamus The part of the brain that produces different body chemicals or hormones.

Imagery Mental pictures. If you calm yourself down by thinking of a peaceful mountain lake, you're using imagery.

Immune system The body's built-in defense network. Any time bacteria or a virus invades the body through a wound or other opening, the body automatically fights the germs off. Most times, the body can combat the germs, but when it can't, you get sick, or a wound becomes infected. See "Human Sexuality."

Impulsive When a person is impulsive, the person is acting on the spur of the moment, without thinking about it too much.

Ingest To take into the body.

Insecurity Not feeling confident about oneself.

GLOSSARY

Insomnia Being unable to sleep.

Interpretation The explanation of something.

Irritability When you are easily annoyed, angered, or made impatient, you are irritable.

Isolation Being totally alone. Sometimes, this means that other people aren't around, but you can be isolated when you're not alone. People who are isolated have no human interaction.

Mental Of or relating to the mind.

Monumental Huge or outstanding.

Mood swings When a person goes from one extreme to another—happy one hour, then depressed the next; or calm for a moment, then extremely annoyed the next—he is said to be having mood swings. Often, mood swings are unusual; the person is unusually happy or unusually anxious.

Nausea An uncomfortable feeling in the stomach like seasickness, accompanied by a distaste for food and the urge to vomit.

Nervous system A network consisting of the brain, spinal cord, and nerves that run throughout the body. The nervous system controls everything we feel. See "Substance Abuse."

Nicotine A powerful, addictive poison found in tobacco smoke. See "Substance Abuse."

Oxygen An invisible, odorless, tasteless gas ("air"). When you breathe, you take oxygen into the bloodstream, which in turn carries it to all parts of the body. See "Nutrition" and "Exercise."

Panic attack A sudden sense of extreme fear and terror. A panic attack makes a person feel as if a situation is life-threatening when it usually isn't. The symptoms include sweating, shortness of breath, faintness, and racing heart beat.

Pathological Abnormal or related to a disease.

Perspiration A fluid secreted by the sweat glands of the skin. By releasing this mixture of water, salt, and body waste, pores in the skin help cool off the body. See "Exercise."

Pesticide A chemical, usually poisonous, used to destroy pests.

Phobia A strong fear of an object, activity, or situation. This fear is usually irrational or unfounded. For example, a person may be extremely afraid of being anywhere near a cat—even though cats rarely cause anyone harm.

Psychologically Mental; of or relating to the mind.

Rampage To rush around in a wild way. Or, a span of violent or reckless behavior.

GLOSSARY

Respiratory system The network that comes into action when you breathe in oxygen and breathe out carbon dioxide. See "Exercise."

Scenario An account of a scene or story. If you told someone the details of your fantasy of becoming a rock star, you would be describing a scenario.

Stimulant A drug that speeds up the body's processes. Caffeine is a stimulant. See "Substance Abuse."

Stress The effect that physical and mental demands have on the body.

Stressors Something that makes a physical or mental demand on the body. A test is mentally demanding; exercise is physically demanding.

Synonymous Similar in meaning. For example, happiness is synonymous with cheerfulness.

Tranquilizer A drug used to calm a person's emotions. See "Substance Abuse."

Tuberculosis A disease of the lungs, passed on by coughing, sneezing, or spitting. See "Substance Abuse."

Ulcer The breaking down and disintegration of skin or tissue. Often, when people use the term ulcer, they mean peptic ulcers, which are open sores on the lining of the stomach.

Vulnerable Open to damage, or liable to be affected by something negative. When you go swimming without wearing a sunscreen, your skin is vulnerable to damaging sun rays.

USEFUL NAMES AND ADDRESSES

Questions you should ask if you call or write any of the associations listed here:
—Am I eligible for your services?
—Is your serice or program free of charge? If there is a cost, how much is it?
—What is your policy concerning confidentiality?

LEARNING AND EDUCATION

The Anxiety Disorders Institute
1 Dunwoody Park
Atlanta, GA 30338
(404) 395-6845

HELP
638 South Street
Philadelphia, PA 19147
(215) 546-7766
"Youth to help Youth"; maintains telephone counseling service, legal, psychological, medical, and referral services.

The Institute of Rational Living
45 East 65th Street
New York, NY 10021
(212) 535-0822

The Jackie Robinson Foundation (JRF)
80 Eighth Avenue
New York, NY 10011
(212) 675-1511
Develops the leadership and achievement potential of minority and urban youth.

Network International
99 Hudson Street, 10th Floor
New York, NY 10013
(212) 219-4550
Designs and organizes youth programs: i.e. City Kids Coalition, City Kids Speak.

HEALTH AND SEXUALITY

Planned Parenthood Federation of America
810 Seventh Avenue
New York, NY 10019
(212) 541-7800

Youth Services, American Red Cross
18th & E Streets NW
Washington, D.C. 20006
(202) 737-8300
Community educational health programs and service opportunities for youth.

ALCOHOL AND DRUGS/SUBSTANCE ABUSE

EDUCATION

Just Say No Foundation
1777 N. California Boulevard
Suite 210
Walnut Creek, CA 94596
(800) 258-2766
Young student clubs dedicated to combating drug abuse among children.

Target—Helping Students Cope with Alcohol and Drugs
P.O. Box 20626
11724 Plaza Circle
Kansas City, MO 64195
(816) 464-5400
A project of the National Federation of State High School Associations. This is a resource center that provides information on chemical abuse and prevention.

ALCOHOL ABUSE

Al-Anon Family Group Headquarters
P.O. Box 862 Midtown Station
New York, NY 10018
(212) 302-7240
For relatives and friends of persons with an alcohol problem. *Alateen* is a division of this organization and is for persons 12–20 whose lives have been adversely affected by someone else's drinking problem, usually a parent.

Target—Helping Students Cope with Alcohol and Drugs
P.O. Box 20626
11724 Plaza Circle
Kansas City, MO 64195
(816) 464-5400
A project of the National Federation of State High School Associations. This is a resource center that provides information on chemical abuse and prevention.

Twin Town Treatment Center
1706 University Avenue
St. Paul, MN 55104
(800) 645-3662

SUBSTANCE ABUSE

Just Say No Foundation
1777 N. California Boulevard
Suite 210
Walnut Creek, CA 94596
(800) 258-2766
Young student clubs dedicated to combating drug abuse among children.

National Cocaine Hotline
P.O. Box 100
332 Springfield Avenue
Summit, NJ 07901
(800) 262-2463

Pride-Action
100 Edgewood Avenue, Suite 1002
Atlanta, GA 30303
(800) 241-9746 (except in GA)
(404) 651-2548 (in GA)
A resource center with current information on drug and substance abuse.

Target—Helping Students Cope with Alcohol and Drugs
P.O. Box 20626
11724 Plaza Circle
Kansas City, MO 64195
(816) 464-5400
A project of the National Federation of State High School Associations. This is a resource center that provides information on chemical abuse and prevention.

DRUNK DRIVING

Students Against Driving Drunk (SADD)
P.O. Box 800
Marlboro, MA 01752
(617) 481-3568

CIGARETTE SMOKING
Contact your local chapter of either the American Cancer Society or the American Lung Association for information on stop-smoking programs in your area.

SUICIDE PREVENTION

Humanistic Mental Health Foundation
P.O. Box 2170
Aptos, CA 95001
(800) 448-8888

Samaritans
500 Commonwealth Avenue
Kenmore Square
Boston, MA 02215
(617) 247-0220

CHILD ABUSE AND ASSAULT

National Center for Missing and Exploited Children
1835 K Street NW
Suite 600
Washington, D.C. 20006
(800) 843-5678

National Child Abuse Hotline
(800) 4-A-CHILD

National Council on Child Abuse and Family Violence
1050 Connecticut Avenue NW
Suite 300
Washington, D.C. 20036
(800) 222-2000 or (818) 914-2814 (in CA)

RUNAWAYS

Children's Rights of America
2069 Indian Rocks Beach Road
Largo, FL 33544
(813) 593-0090
Missing children network.

Home Run Hotline
(800) HIT-HOME

Runaway Hotline
Governor's Office
P.O. Box 12428
Austin, TX 78711
(800) 213-6946
(800) 392-3352 (in TX)
Referral service for callers in need of shelter, transportation, counseling, medical help, legal assistance, and other related services. Will contact friend, family, or relatives if so desired.

LEGAL SERVICES

If you or someone you know needs legal advice, any of the following organizations will be able to help you.

American Civil Liberties Union—Children's Rights Project
132 West 43rd Street
New York, NY 10036
(212) 944-9800

National Legal Resource Center of Children's Advocacy and Protection
1800 M Street NW, 2nd Floor
Washington, D.C. 20036
(202) 331-2250

National Center of Youth Law
1663 Mission Street, 5th Floor
San Francisco, CA 94103
(415) 543-3307
The National Center of Youth Law is a support center for legal services to children and youth.

Operation Sisters United
4604 13th Street NW
Washington, D.C. 20011
(202) 726-7365
Aids teenage girls who have had conflicts with the law.

INDEX

Page numbers in italics refer to captions and illustrations.

Adrenal gland, 102
Ailments, 102
Alarm, as first-stage physical reaction, 43
Alcohol, 35, 47
    brain and liver damage from, *71*
Ambition, 102
American Association of Behavior Therapists, 63
Anger, 44
    daydreaming to diminish, 87
Animals, stress relieved by, *52*
Anxiety disorders, 27, 62–63, 102
    exercise's effect on, *83*
Apathy, 102
Arguments, *26*
Asthma, 53, 102
Athletics
    pre-game stress, *45*
    tension from, *75*
Attitude, in stress tolerance, 20

Bad habits, worsening of, 47
Bedroom, organization of, 73
Behavioral symptoms, 46
    chronic pattern of, *49*
Blind dates, as stressors, 20
Blood, 102
    stress and clotting of, 15
Body
    breakdown of, 53
    long-term stressor effects on, 28
Boredom, daydreaming to relieve, 87
Boyfriends, 25
Brain, alcohol in damage to, *71*
Breaks, *95*
Breathing
    effects of stress on, 53
    exercises, 84–86
    stress and increased rates of, 15

Caffeine, 35, 102
Cancer, 102
    high-stress lifestyles and, 54
Cardiovascular system, 102
Change-it solution, 70–71
Chemicals
    avoidance of, 72–73
    as environmental stressors, 35

Chronic, definition of, 102
Cigarettes, 35, 47
Circulatory system, 102
Cities, stress in, *30–31*
Cocaine, 47
Colds, 53
Colitis, 53, 102
Competition, winning and, *41*
Composure, 102
Constipation, 53, 102
Contemporary, definition of, 102
Control
    staying in, 98
    stress-avoidance and, 76–77
    of thoughts, 81
Counseling, 93
Cousins, Norman, 80
Crisis, definition of, 102
Crisis center hotlines, 93
Cults, 102

Daily problems, 29
Dating, 25, *78*
Daydreaming, *86, 87*
Death of relative, 30
Demands, avoidance of self-imposed, 73
Depressants, 102
Depression, 27
    symptoms of, 57
Diabetes, 54, 102
Diarrhea, 53
Digestion, 43, 53, 103
    effects on, 15
Dilation, definition of, 103
Disease, 30
    humor and, 80
Drugs, 35, 47, 103

Emotional stressors, 27
Emotions, as stress factors, 44
Environmental factors
    avoidance of, 72–73
    stress and, 30
Exercise, *66–67*
    in control of mood disorders, 57
    effects of, 82
Exhaustion, as third-stage physical reaction, 43
Eyes, stress and pupil dilation, 15

Families
    as source of support, *64*
    stress sources in, 26
Fantasies, 87
Fatigue, 103
Fear, 27
Fight-or-flight situations, 19
Financial costs of stress, *18–19*

Friends
    coping and support from, *50–51*
    need for, *56–57*
    as stressors, 22, *27*
Frustration, 44

Genetics, in stress tolerance, 20
Girlfriends, 25
Goose bumps, 103
Go-with-it solution, 82
Groups
    dangers in behavior of, 61
    as stressors, *22–23*

Habits, worsening of, 47
Hair, stress signaled by playing with, *46*
Hands, stress and sweatiness of, *38*
Health, prolonged stress and effects on, 43
Heart, stress and increase in beating rate of, 15, *38*
Heart disease, 53
Heartburn, 53
Heredity, definition of, 103
High blood pressure, 53, 103
Holidays, as stressors, *17*
Holmes, T.H., 36
Hormones, 103
Hostility, 103
Humor, disease and, 80
Hypertension. *See* High blood pressure
Hyperventilation, 53, 103
Hypothalamus, 15, 103

Illness, 30, 53
    humor and, 80
    stress as cause of, 54
Imagery, 103
Immune system, 103
    stress as factor in breakdown of, 53–54
Impatience, 27
Imprisonment, *37, 58*
Impulsiveness, 103
Indigestion, 53
Ingestion, 103
Injuries, 30
Insecurity, 103
Insomnia, 104
Interpretation, definition of, 104
Irritability, 104
Isolation, 33, 89, 104
    methods to combat, *39*
Judgment,
    stress-avoidance and exercise of, 74–75

Kindness, 89

Life changes, 30
Liver, alcohol in damage to, *71*
Loneliness, 33, 89
   methods to combat, *39*
Marijuana, 35
Mental, definition of, 104
Mental breakdown, chronic stress as cause of, *55*
Mind-over-matter solution, 79
Money, 35
Monumental, definition of, 104
Mood disorders, 57
Mood swings, 104
Moving, 30
Muscles, stress in tension of, 15

Nailbiting, 46
National Runaway Hotline, 60
Nausea, 53, 104
Nervous system, 104
   changes from stress in, 15
Nicotine, 35, 47, 104
Niebuhr, Reinhold, *77*
No, ability to say, 76–77
Noise, 30
Nutrients, stress and effect on reserve of, 15
Nutrition, stress and neglect of, 30

Organization, as stress-avoidance tactic, 73
Overcrowding, 30
Oxygen, 104

Panic attacks, 62, 63, 104
Parental molding, in stress tolerance, 20
Past experiences, in stress tolerance, 20
Pathological, definition of, 104
People
   isolation from. *See* Isolation
   pressure from, 32
People support, 89
Personality, stress-prone types, 39
Perspiration, 104
   stress and increase in, 15
Pesticides, 104
Pets, stress relieved by, *52*
Phobias, 62, 63, 104
Physical activity, to relieve stress, 46
Physical illness, 53

Physical reactions, 19
   in heavy-stress situations, 17
   stages of, 43
   from stress, 15
Physical symptoms, 43
Politics, 35
Pollution, 30
Positive thinking, 79
Problems, supportive advice concerning, *92*
Professional help, 93
Psychologists, 93
Psychological, definition of, 104
Psychological symptoms, 44
   anxiety disorders, 62–63
   mood disorders, 57

Rahe, R.H., 36
Rampages, 104
Rebellious behavior, *55*
Relationships
   self-acceptance and, *88*
   supportiveness of, 89
   supportiveness quiz, 90
Relaxation, 89
   plan for, 94
Resistance, as second-stage physical reaction, 43
Respiratory system, 105
   effects of stress on, 53
Running away, *55*
   hotline concerned with, 60
Rush hour, tension during, *62–63*

Scenario, definition of, 105
School, *101*
   as stressor, 22
Self-acceptance, relationships and, *88*
Selye, Hans, 43
Sexual attraction, 25
Shoplifting, *55*
Signals, 43
Sleep, 43
Sleeping pills, 47
Smoking, 35, 47
Social Readjustment Rating Scale, 36–37
Solutions to stress
   change-it, 70–71
   go-with-it, 82
   mind-over-matter, 79
Stimulants, 105
Stress
   behavioral symptoms, 46
   definition of, 105
   financial costs of, *18–19*
   good sides of, 20
   mismanagement of, 94
   as natural life function, 12

   physical signs of, 43
   psychological signs of, 44
   quiz to evaluate, 48–52
   signals, 43
   solutions to. *See* Solutions to stress
   test for, 40
   vulnerability to, 65
Stress level, scale of, 36–37
Stress-avoidance tactics, 72–73
Stressors
   chemical, 35
   definition of, 12, 105
   emotional, 27
   family as, 26
   friends as, *27*
   high-impact types, 20
   holidays as, *17*
   long-term, 28–30
   physical, 30
   recognition of, 16
   self-made, 24–26
   short-term, 28–30
   spacing and pacing of, 72
   tolerance of, 20
   types, 22
Stretching, exercises, 84–86
Substance abuse, 28, 35, *55*
Sugar, 35
Suicide
   coping with, 60
   help for people contemplating, 59
   signals regarding, 59
   among teenagers, 58
Support, people-related, 89
Synonymous, definition of, 105

Talking, stress and aberrant patterns of, 46
Teenagers, suicide among, 58
Tension, physical activity in release of, *83*
Therapy, 93
Thought control, 81
Tranquilizers, 35, 105
Tuberculosis, 54, 105

Ulcers, 43, 53, 105

Violence, 30
Vulnerability, 105

Weight, 28
White blood cells, 53
Winning in competition, *41*
Work, 35
   stressful types of, *41*
Worry, exercise's effect on, *83*